A VOICE OF REASON

Also By Steven J. Conners

THE MADNESS OF POWER SERIES:

Book One: No More Chances

Book Two: A-B-C

Book Three: Heaven on Earth (coming in 2018)

NON-FICTION

A Voice of Reason

A VOICE OF REASON

A CITIZEN'S REFERENCE

Steven J. Conners

STEVEN J. CONNERS | RENO

Credits: All quotations, speeches and lyrics are sourced from www.wikipedia. com. The Declaration of Independence, the United States Constitution and Amendments are sourced from www.archives.gov/founding-docs.

Cover Design © 2018 Jesse S. Conners

A Voice of Reason/ Steven J. Conners. -- 1st ed.

Print Edition ISBN 978-0-9991754-4-6

Kindle Edition ISBN 978-0-9991754-5-3

DEDICATION

To my mother, Jane:

She taught me early that when you believe in something and take action, it will almost certainly happen.

ACTA NON VERBA!

Contents

Preface

FIRST, ALLOW ME TO THANK you for selecting this book. Hopefully you will find it instructive, motivating and enjoyable. Maybe you will even share it with others.

I began writing this book during the last four years of the George W. Bush administration. Strange things happened.

Then, Barack Hussein Obama became our president, and with him we had a set of good ideas to consider. Have his centrist programs been able to correct the years of stress, danger, and corruption that preceded him? Well, I don't think so. But, you'll be the judge.

Now we have the billionaire, narcissist Donald J. Trump and his promises to *Make America Great Again*! Trump is a businessman, a non-politician, an alleged prodigious deal-maker, and also, a great deceiver. This "new manager" is now in charge of the most powerful nation in the world. It's become painfully evident that Trump's administration, in many ways like the previous ones, is full of false assurances and untruthfulness.

Trump, as our president, is merely a figurehead. He is nothing more than a continuation of earlier administrations with a faithful devotion to venality as old as our country. Nothing new. Same old stuff. We just have different players.

In the next election cycle we will likely get the equivalent "political pigs" at the trough, always wanting more than their share, ultimately forgetting the People.

We've got to stop this charade. It doesn't work.

Information, education, hard work and vigilance are still necessary if we are to continue to be a free people. The warnings and statements regarding our loss of freedom and liberty should not be overlooked. We live in a constantly changing and dangerous era. These times call for every person to come to the aid of their country, for our nation is certainly in big trouble!

Some of our founders had the idea that we would have a bloodless revolution (an election) every four years. But what if an unidentified group of people used illegal influence so that their power could last forever? What if our two-party system slowly became one party like in

Mussolini's Italy? Are his dangerous fascist ideas still alive today? What if they wanted to rule us and remove our freedoms and required that we obey them without objection?

That would be the end of that grand experiment in liberty and the end of the United States of America.

More than any time in our history, we must not allow our government to gain absolute power over us or we will quietly lose our freedoms and ultimately become enslaved.

What can each of us do to help maintain our freedoms?

Well, we must use action, not words. *Acta non verba.*

Our leaders, from the top to the bottom, have become very untruthful and can no longer be trusted.

The ideas, herein, will hopefully inspire you to act.

Warning: A powerful and arrogant force is now upon us, considering its own interests, not those of the American people.

History, of course, repeats itself. Much of the egotism and corruption that has plagued mankind throughout the past continues to exist today.

I now quote the late, great George Carlin:

> *If you have selfish, ignorant citizens,*
> *you're gonna' get selfish, ignorant leaders!*

Steven J. Conners
Vista, California
2017

CHAPTER ONE

Famous Americans Speak

WE HAVE ALL QUOTED FAMOUS people and ended up misquoting them. You may often have wanted to use a certain phrase or idea but just couldn't locate it.

In this book, you now have another source for a few choice quotations and a few facts, all in one place. I'll also point out where quotes have been misattributed so often that it's difficult to find them without searching for the wrong source to the quote.

Most of the people I have chosen to quote were Presidents, but I have also included a few others who loved America and certainly contributed their ideas to our history. This selected group of Americans has written and spoken mostly on the subject of liberty. Their comments should remind you of who you are and where those inalienable freedoms came from.

Please take the time to read again the very poignant and sincere words of the people I've selected. The thoughts and intentions of the men and women who created these ideas are truly magnificent and insightful. Many of their comments are filled with common sense and good-old American humor and wit.

The following short biographies and quotations are from many of our greatest Americans and whenever we read their words, we are once again reminded of how important and precious freedom is to all of us.

You might be enthused enough to even read these words aloud to a friend, a child, or a grandchild. After all, most of these magnificent viewpoints were first spoken, before being reduced to writing.

Benjamin Franklin

Born in Boston Massachusetts on January 17 1706, Franklin died on April 17, 1790 in Philadelphia, Pennsylvania. One of the Founding Fathers of America, his wit and wisdom helped the morale of the early freedom fighters. Franklin's portrait is on the $100 bill.

QUOTABLE QUOTES:

Honesty is the best policy.

A small leak will sink a great ship.

Beer is living proof that God loves us and wants us to be happy.

You may delay, but time will not.

A man wrapped up in himself makes a very small bundle.

Rebellion to tyrants is obedience to God.

There has never been or ever will be any such thing as a good war, or a bad peace.

Half the truth is often a great lie.

Those who would give up essential liberty, to purchase a little temporary safety, deserve neither Liberty nor Safety.

Patrick Henry

Born on May 29, 1736 in Hanover County, Virginia -died on June 6, 1799 at Red Hill Plantation, Virginia. He was one of the most outspoken and influential advocates of the American Revolution.

Patrick Henry's speech quoted below was given at Saint John's Church in Richmond, Virginia, on March 23, 1775 to the Virginia House of Burgesses. It first appeared in print in 1817 in Life and Character of Patrick Henry by William Wirt.

QUOTABLE QUOTES:

Gentlemen may cry, peace, peace -- but there is no peace. The war is actually begun! The next gale that sweeps from the north will bring to our ears the clash of resounding arms! Our brethren are already in the field! Why stand we here idle? What is it that the gentlemen wish? What would they have? Is life so dear, or peace so sweet, as to be purchased at the price of chains and slavery? Forbid it, Almighty God! I know not what course others may take; but as for me, give me liberty or give me death!

The Constitution is not an instrument for the government to restrain the people, it is an instrument for the people to restrain the government – lest it come to dominate our lives and interests.

Taxation without representation is tyranny.

If this be treason, make the most of it.

United we stand, divided we fall. Let us not split into factions which must destroy that union upon which our existence hangs.

Thomas Paine

Born January 29, 1737 in Thetford, England--died on June 8, 1809 in New York City, New York. An early American writer, journalist and pamphleteer he was an outspoken supporter of freedom and the Revolution.

Thomas Paine published *The Crisis*, in 1776. It began:

> *These are the times that try men's souls. The summer soldier and the sunshine patriot will, in this crisis, shrink from the service of their country; but he that stands it now, deserves the love and thanks of man and woman. Tyranny, like hell, is not easily conquered...*

QUOTABLE QUOTES:

Government, even in its best state, is but a necessary evil; in its worst state an intolerable one.

If we do not hang together, we shall surely hang separately.

I do not believe in [any] doctrine professed by any church that I know of. My own mind is my own church. All national institutions of churches, [are] human inventions, set up to terrify and enslave mankind, and monopolize power and profit.

Lead, follow, or get out of the way.

That government is best which governs least.

Alexander Hamilton

Born January 11, 1755 in the West Indies– died on July 12, 1804 in Weehawken, New Jersey following injuries sustained in a duel with Aaron Burr. Alexander Hamilton's portrait is on the $10 bill.

QUOTABLE QUOTES:

The people are turbulent and changing; they seldom judge or determine right. Give therefore to the first class a distinct permanent share in the government. Can a democratic assembly who annually revolve in the mass of the people be supposed steadily to pursue the public good?

Man is a reasoning, rather than a reasonable animal.

In framing a government which is to be administered by men over men the great difficulty lies in this: You must first enable the government to control the governed, and in the next place, oblige it to control itself.

Real firmness is good for anything; strut is good for nothing.

In the general course of human nature, a power over a man's subsistence.

James Madison

Born on March 16, 1751 in Port Conway, Virginia – died on June 28, 1836 in Montpelier, Virginia. He was the 4th President of the United States. James Madison's portrait was on the $5,000 bill.

QUOTABLE QUOTES:

All men having power ought to be mistrusted.

Knowledge will forever govern ignorance; and a people who mean to be their own governors must arm themselves with the power which knowledge gives.

I believe there are more instances of the abridgement of freedom of the people by gradual and silent encroachments by those in power than by violent and sudden usurpations.

The Constitution preserves the advantage of being armed, which Americans possess over the people of almost every other nation where the governments are afraid to trust the people with arms.

If Tyranny and Oppression come to this land, it will be in the guise of fighting a foreign enemy.

The executive [President] has no right, in any case, to decide the question, whether there is or is not cause for declaring war.

George Washington

Born February 22, 1732 in Popes Creek Plantation, in Westmoreland County, Virginia--died on December 14, 1799. Washington was the 1st president of the United States and is called the Father of Our Country. Washington's image is part of the Mount Rushmore National Memorial and the Washington Monument in Washington, D.C with his portrait on the U.S. $1 bill.

QUOTABLE QUOTES:

Arbitrary power is most easily established on the ruins of liberty abused to licentiousness.

Few men have virtue to withstand the highest bidder.

Observe good faith and justice toward all nations. Cultivate peace and harmony with all.

It is our true policy to steer clear of entangling dalliances with any portion of the foreign world.

My first wish is to see this plague of mankind, war, banished from the earth.

If the freedom of speech is taken away then dumb and silent we may be led, like sheep to the slaughter.

John Adams

Born in Braintree, Massachusetts on October 30, 1735 –died on July 4, 1826. He was the 2nd president of the United States. At ninety years old he is the longest living person to be President. Adams died at Quincy, Massachusetts after uttering the famous last words "Thank God, Thomas Jefferson still survives." Unbeknownst to Adams, Jefferson had died a few hours earlier.

QUOTABLE QUOTES:

The Hebrews have done more to civilize men than any other nation...[I believe] the Jews to be the most essential instrument for civilizing the nations.

Abuse of words has been the great instrument of sophistry and chicanery, of party, faction, and division of society.

Fear is the foundation of most governments.

Democracy, while it lasts, is more bloody than either aristocracy or monarchy. Remember, democracy never lasts long. It soon wastes, exhausts, and murders itself. There is never a democracy that did not commit suicide.

Power always thinks that it is doing God's service when it is violating all His laws.

Great is the guilt of an unnecessary war.

Thomas Jefferson

Born in Shadwell, Virginia on April 13, 1743–died on July 4, 1826. He was the 3rd president of the United States. On July 4, 1826, the 50th anniversary of the Declaration of Independence, he died at his home, Monticello, a few hours ahead of his friend John Adams. His image is on the Mount Rushmore National Memorial and the Jefferson Memorial in Washington, D.C. His portrait appears on the U.S. $2 bill.

QUOTABLE QUOTES:

I am mortified to be told that, in the United States of America, the sale of a book can become a subject of inquiry, and of criminal inquiry too.

Conquest is not in our principles. It is inconsistent with our government.

All tyranny needs to gain a foothold is for people of good conscience to remain silent.

If there is one principle more deeply rooted in the mind of every American, it is that we should have nothing to do with conquest.

I sincerely believe that banking establishments are more dangerous than standing armies, and that the principle of spending money to be paid by posterity, under the name of funding, is but swindling futurity on a large scale.

Every generation needs a new revolution.

If God is just, I tremble for my country.

Abraham Lincoln

Born on February 12, 1809 in Hardin County, Kentucky – died on April 15, 1865 in Washington, DC. He was the 16th President of the United States and the first president from the Republican Party. Lincoln was assassinated On April 14, 1865. Lincoln's image is part of the Mount Rushmore National Memorial and the Lincoln Memorial in Washington, D.C with his portrait on the U.S. $5 bill.

QUOTABLE QUOTES:

Discourage litigation. Persuade your neighbors to compromise whenever you can. As a peacemaker the lawyer has superior opportunity of being a good man. There will still be business enough.

Better to remain silent and be thought a fool than to speak out and remove all doubt.

If once you forfeit the confidence of your fellow-citizens, you can never regain their respect and esteem.

You can fool all the people some of the time, and some of the people all the time, but you cannot fool all the people all the time.

Our safety, our liberty, depends upon preserving the Constitution of the United States as our fathers made it inviolate. The people of the United States are the rightful masters of both Congress and the courts, not to overthrow the Constitution, but to overthrow the men who pervert the Constitution.

A house [nation] divided against itself cannot stand.

Mark Twain

Born Samuel Langhorne Clemens (pseudonym Mark Twain) on November 30, 1835 in Florida, Missouri and died on April 21, 1910 in Hartford, Connecticut. A celebrated American writer, journalist and humorist, he had much to say.

QUOTABLE QUOTES:

Always do right. This will gratify some people and astonish the rest.

Get your facts first, then you can distort them as you please.

Go to Heaven for the climate, Hell for the company.

A person who won't read has no advantage over one who can't read.

There is no distinctly American criminal class - except Congress.

There are lies, damned lies and statistics.

Suppose you were an idiot, and suppose you were a member of Congress; but I repeat myself.

Denial ain't just a river in Egypt.

Loyalty to the country always. Loyalty to the government when it deserves it.

Theodore Roosevelt

Born October 27, 1858 in New York and died on Jan. 6, 1919 in Oyster Bay, New York. He was Vice President under President McKinley. When McKinley was assassinated he became the 26th president of the United States. His image is on the Mount Rushmore National Memorial.

QUOTABLE QUOTES:

To educate a man in mind and not in morals is to educate a menace to society.

No man is above the law, and no man is below it.

The government is us; we are the government, you and me.

Every immigrant who comes here should be required within five years to learn English or leave the country.

No man is justified in doing evil on the ground of expedience.

When they call the roll in the Senate, the Senators do not know whether to answer "Present" or "Not guilty."

To announce that there must be no criticism of the president, is morally treasonable to the American public.

Woodrow Wilson

Born in Staunton, Virginia December 28, 1856 and died on February 3, 1924 in Washington, DC. Woodrow Wilson was the 28th president of the United States and the founder of the League of Nations.

QUOTABLE QUOTES:

The seed of revolution is repression.

America was established not to create wealth but to realize a vision, to realize an ideal - to discover and maintain liberty among men.

A conservative is a man who just sits and thinks; mostly sits.

I have long enjoyed the friendship and companionship of Republicans because I am by instinct a teacher, and I would like to teach them something.

The history of liberty is a history of resistance.

The American Revolution was a beginning, not a consummation

If there are men in this country big enough to own the government of the United States, they are going to own it.

Will Rogers

Born William Penn Adair Rogers on November 4, 1879 on the Cherokee Nation in Oologah, Oklahoma—died on August 15, 1935 in Alaska and is buried in Claremore, Oklahoma. He was first an Indian, a cowboy and then a national figure.

QUOTABLE QUOTES:

George Washington would sue us for calling him "father."

Be thankful we're not getting all the government we're paying for.

Ancient Rome declined because it had a Senate, now what's going to happen to us with both a House and a Senate?

Advertising is the art of convincing people to spend money they don't have for something they don't need.

You can't say civilization don't advance... In every war they kill you in a new way.

About all I can say for the United States Senate is that it opens with a prayer and closes with an investigation.

I am not a member of any organized political party. I am a Democrat.

Louis D. Brandeis

Born Louis Dembitz Brandeis on November 13, 1856 in Louisville, KY and died on October 5, 1941 in Dedham, Massachusetts. A famous American Supreme Court Justice, a litigator, an advocate of privacy and the author of the Brandeis Brief. He was the first Jewish Supreme Court Justice in American history.

QUOTABLE QUOTES:

America has believed that in differentiation, not in uniformity, lies the path of progress. It acted on this belief; it has advanced human happiness, and it has prospered.

Fear of serious injury alone cannot justify oppression of free speech and assembly. Men feared witches and burnt women. It is the function of speech to free men from the bondage of irrational fears.

We can have democracy in this country, or we can have great wealth concentrated in the hands of a few, but we can't have both.

Neutrality is at time a graver sin than belligerence.

Our government teaches the whole people by its example. If the government becomes the lawbreaker, it breeds contempt for law; it invites every man to become a law unto himself; it invites anarchy.

Franklin Delano Roosevelt

Born in 1882 at Hyde Park, New York—died on April 12, 1945, in Warm Springs, Georgia. FDR (Franklin Delano Roosevelt) was the 32nd president of the United States and was elected to 4 terms in office from 1933 to 1945.

QUOTABLE QUOTES:

The only thing we have to fear is fear itself.

Here is my principle: Taxes shall be levied according to ability to pay. That is the only American principle.

Human kindness has never weakened the stamina or softened the fiber of a free people. A nation does not have to be cruel to be tough.

In politics, nothing happens by accident. If it happens, you can bet it was planned that way.

More than an end to war, we want an end to the beginning of all wars - yes, an end to this brutal, inhuman and thoroughly impractical method of settling the differences between governments.

The liberty of a democracy is not safe if the people tolerate the growth of private power to a point where it becomes stronger than their democratic state itself. That, in its essence, is fascism - ownership of government by an individual, by a group, or any controlling private power.

Sir Winston Spencer Churchill

Born on November 30, 1874 at Blenheim Palace in Oxfordshire, England – died at Kensington, London, England on January 24, 1965. Appointed Prime Minister of The United Kingdom in 1940 and remained in this position until 1945 only to return to the office in 1951 until 1955. Churchill brilliantly guided England through WWII and saw many changes in the United Kingdom.

QUOTABLE QUOTES:

The price of greatness is responsibility.

I like things to happen, if they don't happen I like to make them happen.

Never give in, never, never, never, never – in nothing great or small, large or petty – never give in, except to convictions of honor and good sense.

A lady came up to me one day said: 'Sir! You are drunk.' To which I replied: 'I am drunk today madam, and tomorrow I shall be sober, but you will still be ugly.

He has all the virtues I dislike and none of the vices I admire.

I have nothing to offer but blood, toil, tears and sweat.

We shall go on to the end. We shall fight in France, we shall fight on the seas and oceans, we shall fight with growing strength in the air, we shall defend our island, whatever the cost may be. We shall fight on the beaches we shall fight on the landing grounds, we shall fight in the hills; we shall never surrender!

Dorothy Thompson

Born in Lancaster, New York, on July 9, 1894 - died in Lisbon, Portugal, on January 30, 1961. American writer and outspoken journalist affectionately known as the "Blue-Eyed Tornado." She was married to author Sinclair Lewis.

<u>QUOTABLE QUOTES:</u>

I don't want to emphasize American unity if America is unified around a bad idea.

Society is deranged. It is dominated by moral and emotional morons...I want sabotage and opposition... sabotage and opposition...sabotage and opposition, against militarism in all of its forms.

We are being subjected day after day to flat lies. The end result will be either a public doped into indifference [or] provoked into war.

No people ever recognize their dictator in advance. He never stands for election on the platform of dictatorship. He always represents himself as the instrument [of] the Incorporated National Will. When our dictator turns up you can depend on it that he will be one of the boys, and he will stand for everything traditionally American. And nobody will ever say 'Heil' to him, nor will they call him 'Führer'' or 'Duce.' But they will greet him with one great big, universal, democratic, sheep-like bleat of 'O.K., Chief! Fix it like you wanna, Chief! Oh Kaaaay!'

When Liberty is taken away by force, it can be restored by force. When it is relinquished voluntarily, by default, it can never be recovered.

Ayn Rand

Born Alissa Zinovievna Rosenbaum on February 2, 1905 of a Jewish family in Saint Petersburg, Russia—died on March 6, 1982 in New York City. A writer. Her philosophy and fiction both emphasize the concepts of individualism and rational egoism. She believed in the individual.

QUOTABLE QUOTES:

That man must choose his values and actions by reason; That the individual has a right to exist for his own sake, neither sacrificing self to others nor others to self; That no one has the right to seek values from others by physical force or impose ideas on others by physical force.

Do not ever say that the desire to "do good" by force is a good motive. Neither power-lust nor stupidity are good motives.

Achieving life is not the equivalent of avoiding death.

Force and mind are opposites; morality ends where a gun begins.

A government is the most dangerous threat to man's rights: it holds a legal monopoly on the use of physical force against legally disarmed victims.

The only power any government has is the power to crack down on criminals. Well, when there aren't enough criminals, one makes them. One declares so many things to be a crime that it becomes impossible for men to live without breaking laws.

Eleanor Roosevelt

Born Anna Eleanor Roosevelt on October 11, 1884, New York, New York--died November 7, 1962, New York, New York. The niece of President Theodore Roosevelt and wife of President Franklin D. Roosevelt, Eleanor was a diplomat and humanitarian and one of the world's most widely admired and powerful women.

QUOTABLE QUOTES:

Do what you feel in your heart to be right- for you'll be criticized anyway. You'll be damned if you do, and damned if you don't.

For it isn't enough to talk about peace. One must believe in it. And it isn't enough to believe in it. One must work at it.

It is better to light a candle than curse the darkness.

It is not more vacation we need—it is more vocation.

No one can make you feel inferior without your consent.

Women are like teabags. We don't know our true strength until we are in hot water!

You must do the things you think you cannot do.

Hate and force cannot be in just a part of the world without having an effect on the rest of it.

Harry S. Truman

Born in Lamar, Missouri, in 1884—died on December 26, 1972 in Independence, Missouri. He was the 33rd president of the United States. He assumed office at the death of FDR on April 12, 1945 and gave the order to drop the atomic bombs on Japan on August 6, 1945.

QUOTABLE QUOTES:

The buck stops here!

A politician is a man who understands government. A statesman is a politician who's been dead for 15 years.

I never did give anybody hell. I just told the truth, they thought it was hell.

If you can't stand the heat, get out of the kitchen.

You want a friend in Washington? Get a dog.

It's a recession when your neighbor loses his job; it's a depression when you lose yours.

Richard Nixon is a no good, lying bastard. He can lie out of both sides of his mouth at the same time, and if he ever caught himself telling the truth, he'd lie just to keep his hand in.

My choice early in life was either to be a piano-player in a whorehouse or be a politician. And to tell the truth, there's hardly any difference.

When even one American - who has done nothing wrong - is forced by fear to shut his mind and close his mouth - then all Americans are in peril.

Dwight D. Eisenhower

Born in 1890 in Denison, Texas--died on March 28, 1969 in Washington, DC. He was the 34th president of the United States. During WWII he was the Supreme Commander of all Allied Forces.

QUOTABLE QUOTES:

I hate war as only a soldier who has lived it can, only as one who has seen its brutality, its futility, its stupidity.

When people speak to you about a preventive war, you tell them to go and fight it. After my experience, I have come to hate war.

I think that people want peace so much that one of these days government had better get out of their way and let them have it.

In most communities it is illegal to cry "fire" in a crowded assembly. Should it not be considered serious international misconduct to manufacture a general war scare in an effort to achieve local political aims?

War settles nothing. ...We will bankrupt ourselves in the vain search for absolute security.

Any man who wants to be president is either an egomaniac or crazy.

We must guard against the acquisition of unwarranted influence, whether sought or unsought, by the military-industrial complex. The potential for the disastrous rise of misplaced power exists and will persist.

Edward R. Murrow

Born Edward Roscoe Murrow on April 25, 1908 in Polecat Creek, North Carolina—died on April 27, 1965 in New York City, New York. An American radio and TV commentator who is credited for single-handedly creating the concept of broadcast-journalism.

QUOTABLE QUOTES:

Anyone who isn't confused really doesn't understand the situation.

Everyone is a prisoner of his own experiences. No one can eliminate prejudices - just recognize them.

No one can terrorize a whole nation—unless we are all his accomplices.

To be persuasive we must be believable; to be believable we must be credible; to be credible we must be truthful.

We cannot defend freedom abroad by deserting it at home.

Just because your voice reaches halfway around the world doesn't mean you are wiser than when it reached only to the end of the bar.

We must not confuse dissent with disloyalty. When the loyal opposition dies, I think the soul of America dies with it.

Good night, and good luck.

John Fitzgerald Kennedy

Born May 29, 1917 in Brookline, Massachusetts – assassinated November 22, 1963 in Dallas, Texas. Known as JFK, he was the 35th President of the United States. Considered an icon of American liberalism.

QUOTABLE QUOTES:

Do you realize the responsibility I carry? I'm the only person standing between Richard Nixon and the White House.

I think this is the most extraordinary collection of talent, of human knowledge, that has ever been gathered at the White House—with the possible exception of when Thomas Jefferson dined alone.

If a free society cannot help the many who are poor, it cannot save the few who are rich.

Mankind must put an end to war, or war will put an end to mankind.

The basic problems facing the world today are not susceptible to a military solution.

The very word 'secrecy' is repugnant in a free and open society; and we are as a people inherently and historically opposed to secret societies, to secret oaths, and to secret proceedings.

Those who make peaceful revolution impossible will make violent revolution inevitable.

And so, my fellow Americans, ask not what your country can do for you; ask what you can do for your country.

Lyndon B. Johnson

Born on August 27, 1908, in Johnson City, Texas—died on January 22, 1973 in Stonewall, Texas. He was elected as JFK's Vice President. After Kennedy's assassination in 1963 he became the 36th President.

QUOTABLE QUOTES:

Did you ever think that making a speech on economics is a lot like pissing down your leg? It seems hot to you, but it never does to anyone else.

I never trust a man unless I've got his pecker in my pocket.

It is important that the United States remain a two-party system. I'm a fellow who likes small parties and the Republican Party can't be too small to suit me.

I don't know what it will take out there—500 casualties maybe, maybe 500,000. It's the oughts that scare me.

The guns and bombs, the rockets and the warships, all are symbols of human failure.

If one little old general in shirtsleeves can take Saigon, think about 200 million Chinese comin' down those trails. No sir, I don't want to fight them.

They call upon us to supply American boys to do the job that Asian boys should do.

Martin Luther King, Jr.

Born Michael Luther King, Jr. on May 29, 1929 in Atlanta, Georgia - assassinated on April 4, 1968 in Memphis, Tennessee. King is considered the greatest civil rights leader of the 20th century.

QUOTABLE QUOTES:

A man can't ride your back unless it's bent.

Before the Pilgrims landed at Plymouth, we were here. Before the pen of Jefferson etched across the pages of history the majestic words of the Declaration of Independence, we were here. If the inexpressible cruelties of slavery could not stop us, the opposition we now face will surely fail.

I want to be the white man's brother, not his brother-in-law.

The hottest place in Hell is reserved for those who remain neutral in times of great moral conflict.

War is a poor chisel to carve out tomorrow.

We may have all come on different ships, but we're in the same boat now.

We must learn to live together as brothers or perish together as fools.

Never forget that everything Hitler did in Germany was legal.

Robert Francis Kennedy

Born November 20, 1925 in Brookline, Massachusetts - assassinated on June 5, 1968 in Los Angeles, California. Known as RFK he was the brother of President of John F. Kennedy and Attorney General of the United States. He was great leader for justice, truth and freedom.

QUOTABLE QUOTES:

I thought they'd get one of us, but Jack, after all he's been through, never worried about it. I thought it would be me.

But suppose God is black? What if we go to Heaven and we, all our lives, have treated the Negro as an inferior, and God is there, and we look up and He is not white? What then is our response?

I believe that, as long as there is plenty, poverty is evil.

One-fifth of the people are against everything all the time.

People say I am ruthless. I am not ruthless. And if I find the man who is calling me ruthless, I shall destroy him.

Whenever men take the law into their own hands, the loser is the law. And when the law loses, freedom languishes.

There are those who look at things the way they are, and ask why...I dream of things that never were, and ask why not?

Richard Milhous Nixon

Born on January 9, 1913 in Yorba Linda, California-died on April 22, 1994 in New York City, New York. He was the 37th President of the United States. His vice president, Spiro Agnew resigned, and in 1974, following the Watergate Scandal, Richard Nixon became the only president to resign.

QUOTABLE QUOTES:

Nobody is a friend of ours. Let's face it.

It's the responsibility of the media to look at the president with a microscope, but they go too far when they use a proctoscope.

The press is the enemy.

Well, I screwed it up real good, didn't I? ...I brought myself down. I impeached myself by resigning.

You won't have Nixon to kick around anymore because, gentlemen, this is my last press conference.

Under the doctrine of separation of powers, the manner in which the president personally exercises his assigned executive powers is not subject to questioning by another branch of government.

When the President does it that means that it's not illegal.

I am not a crook.

Jimmy Carter

Born James Earl Carter. Jr. on October 1, 1924 in Plaines, Georgia. He was elected the 39th President of the United States in 1977 and became a Nobel Peace laureate in 2002.

America did not invent human rights. In a very real sense human rights invented America.

For the first time in the history of our country the majority of our people believe that the next five years will be worse than the past five years.

Human rights are the soul of our foreign policy, because human rights are the very soul of our sense of nationhood.

There should be an honest attempt at the reconciliation of differences before resorting to combat.

Republicans are men of narrow vision, who are afraid of the future.

We will not learn to live together in peace by killing each other's children.

I thought then, and I think now, that the invasion of Iraq was unnecessary and unjust. And I think the premises on which it was launched were false.

Ronald W. Reagan

Ronald Wilson Reagan was born February 6, 1911 in Tampico, Illinois—died on June 5, 2004 in Los Angeles, California. He was the 40th President of the United States.

QUOTABLE QUOTES:

You can tell a lot about a fellow's character by his way of eating jellybeans.

Before I refuse to take your questions, I have an opening statement.

Government's first duty is to protect the people, not run their lives.

How can a president not be an actor?

Politics I supposed to be the second-oldest profession. I have come to realize that it bears a very close resemblance to the first.

I have left orders to be awakened at any time in case of national emergency, even if I'm in a cabinet meeting.

A people free to choose will always choose peace.

No mother would ever willingly sacrifice her sons for territorial gain, for economic advantage, for ideology.

Maya Angelou

Born Marguerite Johnson in St. Louis, Missouri, on April 4, 1928. She is an author, poet, historian, songwriter, playwright, dancer, stage and screen producer, director, performer, singer, and civil rights activist.

QUOTABLE QUOTES:

Achievement brings its own anticlimax.

As far as I knew white women were never lonely, except in books. White men adored them, Black men desired them, and Black women worked for them.

At fifteen, life had taught me undeniably that surrender, in its place, was as honorable as resistance, especially if one had no choice.

Bitterness is like cancer. It eats upon the host. But anger is like fire. It burns it all clean.

Any book that helps a child to form a habit of reading, to make reading one of his deep and continuing needs, is good for him.

All men are prepared to accomplish the incredible if their ideals are threatened.

George Herbert Walker Bush

Born on June 12, 1924 in Milton, Massachusetts, he was Vice President under President Ronald Reagan and then became the 41st President of the United States of America. Previously, Bush was an ambassador to the United Nations, Republican National Committee chairman and Director of the Central Intelligence Agency.

QUOTABLE QUOTES:

It's a very good question, very direct, and I'm not going to answer it.

I am not one who—who flamboyantly believes in throwing a lot of words around.

I have opinions of my own, strong opinions, but I don't always agree with them.

I'll be glad to reply to or dodge your questions, depending on what I think will help our election most.

It's no exaggeration to say that the un-decideds could go one-way or another.

You cannot be President of the United States if you don't have faith. I remember Lincoln, going to his knees in times of trial in the Civil War... and all that stuff.

Please don't ask me to do that which I've just said I'm not going to do, because you're burning up time. The meter is running through the sand on you, and I am now filibustering.

Bill Clinton

Born William Jefferson Blythe III on August 19, 1946 in Hope, Arkansas, he was the 42nd President of the United States. Presenting himself as a moderate and a member of the New Democrat wing of the Democratic Party, he is known affectionately as "Slick Willy" and oversaw the longest peacetime economic expansion in history.

QUOTABLE QUOTES:

You know, everybody makes mistakes when they are president.

I like the job. That's what I'll miss the most... I'm not sure anybody ever liked this as much as I've liked it.

In today's knowledge-based economy, what you earn depends on what you learn. Jobs in the information technology sector, for example, pay 85 percent more than the private sector average.

Let me say this as clearly as I can: No matter how sharp a grievance or how deep a hurt, there is no justification for killing innocents.

Never pick a fight with people who buy ink by the barrel.

We must teach our children to resolve their conflicts with words, not weapons.

Today, many companies are reporting that their number one constraint on growth is the inability to hire workers with the necessary skills.

George W. Bush

Born July 6, 1946 in New Haven, CT and was the 43rd President of the United States and ex-governor of Texas. He is the son of former President George H. W. Bush and is the second president to be the son of a former United States president (the first was John Quincy Adams) George W. Bush is considered by some to be the worst president in the history of the United States of America.

QUOTABLE QUOTES:

To those of you who received honors, awards and distinctions, I say well done. To the 'C' students, you, too, can be president of the United States.

Our Nation must defend the sanctity of marriage.

I just want you to know that, when we talk about war, we're really talking about peace.

It isn't pollution that's harming the environment. It's the impurities in our air and water that are doing it.

I think war is a dangerous place. Bring 'em on!

Our nation is somewhat sad, but we're angry. There's a certain level of blood lust, but we won't let it drive our reaction. We're steady, clear-eyed and patient, but pretty soon we'll have to start displaying scalps.

You can fool some of the people all the time, and those are the ones you want to concentrate on.

Barack H. Obama

Born August 4, 1961 in Honolulu, Hawaii and is the 44th President of the United States and former US Senator from Illinois. He is the first African-American to hold this office and inherited from the G.W. Bush administration and a huge national debt, a failing economy and wars in two nations. Obama enacted many good social programs.

QUOTABLE QUOTES:

Al Qaeda is still a threat. We cannot pretend somehow that because Barack Hussein Obama got elected as president, suddenly everything is going to be OK.

We have an obligation and a responsibility to be investing in our students and our schools. We must make sure that people who have the grades, the desire and the will, but not the money, can still get the best education possible.

Change will not come if we wait for some other person or some other time. We are the ones we've been waiting for. We are the change that we seek.

There's not a liberal America and a conservative America— there's the United States of America.

I found this national debt, doubled, wrapped in a big bow waiting for me as I stepped into the Oval Office.

What Washington needs is adult supervision.

Donald J. Trump

Born June 14, 1946 in Jamaica, Queens, New York he is the 45th President of the United States and former CEO of The Trump Organization. He is a businessperson and a non- politician. His campaign promises have divided the nation. He has been labeled an egotistical man who says wild and precarious things. Trump intends to undo most of the programs put into place by his predecessors. Unfortunately, there is surely more to come, but the following are some of the quotes in President Trump's first days in office.

QUOTABLE QUOTES:

The beauty of me is that I'm very rich.

I have been very successful. People love me. And you know what, everybody loves me.

I don't like losers.

My IQ is one of the highest—and you all know it! Please don't feel so stupid or insecure; it's not your fault.

I will build a great wall—and nobody builds walls better than me, believe me – and I'll build them very inexpensively. I will build a great, great wall on our southern border, and I will make Mexico pay for that wall. Mark my words.

You know, I'm automatically attracted to beautiful—I just start kissing them. It's like a magnet. Just kiss. I don't even wait. And when you're a star, they let you do it. You can do anything. ...Grab them by the pussy. You can do anything!

The previous pages have reflected just a few of the hundreds of people who have helped to shape our lives. I'm quite sure that all of these Americans were as extraordinary as history has reported them to be.

The individuals that I selected are some of my favorites, but in reality, how do you condense the biographies and quotations of such a group into a few pages? During their lifetimes, these Americans declared a belief in our country and its people. Their words express an emotion that seems to be ageless. Even today, their ideas and observations are still fresh and full of spirit.

Through the years, we have found in these unique and devoted people a voice that is in every sense, American. These great citizens have articulated thoughts that continue to inspire and remind us who we are, of the country in which we live, and where it all came from. Their eloquence and sincerity certainly make us thankful to be citizens of the United States of America. Their words were the truth as they saw it during their lifetimes. The inherited wisdom from these people and their words are lasting encouragement and will forever be meaningful and helpful to future generations.

Each of these thinkers has had many books and articles written about their lives. I suggest that if some of the quotes have sparked an interest in these great Americans, you should get a book, or go online to learn more.

Maybe we should take the time to compare the indispensable ideas from these great Americans against the current ersatz half-truths our government and their obliging media are feeding us. The truth, today, is very hard to find.

Sometimes we tend to forget how our country began and how a small group of men created the precious documents that have allowed you, and your family, to live in this land of the free for over 240 years. These were not mere words, but the magnificent ideas and feelings that flowed from the collective thinking and heated debates of our Founding Fathers. It is their unique concept of how a new government, "Of the People, By the People and For the People," might be created.

The United States of America was the first legitimate experiment in "People Rule." Even though the original ideas of freedom have been around for thousands of years, we were the first to use these ideas for an entire nation.

So, how did these ideas of freedom for our great country come about? Well, it seems to have all started many years before the actual revolutionary days, notably, with the thoughts and conversations of James Madison, John Adams and Thomas Jefferson.

During the writing of the Declaration of Independence, Jefferson and the founding fathers looked for precedents, in order to declare freedom from King George III. They discovered an example in a pronouncement that was made 561 years earlier, on the plains of Runnymede, England.

The concept of the people telling its ruling authority that certain things would not be tolerated was the basis of historic change. The people resisted and opposed the King.

King John's disastrous foreign policies culminated in a lost battle with King Philip II of France, causing King John to forfeit the French territory that he had inherited. When John returned to England he was broke and he immediately attempted to rebuild his coffers by enforcing scutage (taxation) from the barons who had not participated in his war with France.

His barons refused. They could not endure more taxes. They protested and were adamant that King John should adhere to the previous ideas limiting his ability to demand funds. They insisted on a reconfirmation of the Coronation Oath that was made by Henry I in 1100. In that oath Henry declared that there would be certain limitations on how even a king could gather funds from the people.

On June 15, 1215 the barons came together as a group to complain and require that the despotic and cash-poor King John recognize their rights. At the end of the day, the barons won and the written document they had created went forth under royal seal and was read to all freemen throughout the country.

This important leap for liberty was called the Magna Carta (Great Charter) and there is little doubt that this document would later become the necessary inspiration for our own Declaration of Independence.

Again, we are living in "times that will try men's souls."

The next few pages contain the magnificent words of our celebrated Declaration of Independence as written by Thomas Jefferson. In revisiting this and the other great national documents remind us how privileged we all are to live in a land that is Free.

After reading these meaningful words, you might remember that as an American Citizen, you have the power, the right, and the responsibility to change all issues concerning your life and the lives of your fellow Americans.

CHAPTER TWO

The Declaration of Independence

Note: The following text is a transcription of the Stone Engraving of the parchment Declaration of Independence (the document on display in the Rotunda at the National Archives Museum.) The spelling and punctuation reflects the original.

IN CONGRESS, JULY 4, 1776.

The unanimous Declaration of the thirteen united States of America, When in the Course of human events, it becomes necessary for one people to dissolve the political bands which have connected them with another, and to assume among the powers of the earth, the separate and equal station to which the Laws of Nature and of Nature's God entitle them, a decent respect to the opinions of mankind requires that they should declare the causes which impel them to the separation.

We hold these truths to be self-evident, that all men are created equal, that they are endowed by their Creator with certain unalienable Rights, that among these are Life, Liberty and the pursuit of Happiness.--That to secure these rights, Governments are instituted among Men, deriving their just powers from the consent of the governed, --That whenever any Form of Government becomes destructive of these ends, it is the Right of the People to alter or to abolish it, and to institute new Government, laying its foundation on such principles and organizing its powers in such form, as to them shall seem most likely to effect their Safety and Happiness. Prudence, indeed, will dictate that Governments long established should not be changed for light and transient causes; and accordingly all experience hath shewn, that mankind are more disposed to suffer, while evils are sufferable, than to right themselves by abolishing the forms to which they are accustomed. But when a long train of abuses and usurpations, pursuing invariably the same Object evinces a design to reduce them under absolute Despotism, it is their right, it is their duty, to throw off such Government, and to provide new Guards for their future security.--Such has been the patient sufferance of these Colonies; and such is now the necessity which constrains them to alter their former Systems of Government. The history of the present King of Great Britain is a history of repeated injuries and usurpations, all having in direct object the establishment of an absolute Tyranny over these States. To prove this, let Facts be submitted to a candid world.

He has refused his Assent to Laws, the most wholesome and necessary for the public good.

He has forbidden his Governors to pass Laws of immediate and pressing importance, unless suspended in their operation till his Assent should be obtained; and when so suspended, he has utterly neglected to attend to them.

He has refused to pass other Laws for the accommodation of large districts of people, unless those people would relinquish the right of Representation in the Legislature, a right inestimable to them and formidable to tyrants only.

He has called together legislative bodies at places unusual, uncomfortable, and distant from the depository of their public Records, for the sole purpose of fatiguing them into compliance with his measures.

He has dissolved Representative Houses repeatedly, for opposing with manly firmness his invasions on the rights of the people.

He has refused for a long time, after such dissolutions, to cause others to be elected; whereby the Legislative powers, incapable of Annihilation, have returned to the People at large for their exercise; the State remaining in the mean time exposed to all the dangers of invasion from without, and convulsions within.

He has endeavoured to prevent the population of these States; for that purpose obstructing the Laws for Naturalization of Foreigners; refusing to pass others to encourage their migrations hither, and raising the conditions of new Appropriations of Lands.

He has obstructed the Administration of Justice, by refusing his Assent to Laws for establishing Judiciary powers.

He has made Judges dependent on his Will alone, for the tenure of their offices, and the amount and payment of their salaries.

He has erected a multitude of New Offices, and sent hither swarms of Officers to harrass our people, and eat out their substance.

He has kept among us, in times of peace, Standing Armies without the Consent of our legislatures.

He has affected to render the Military independent of and superior to the Civil power.

He has combined with others to subject us to a jurisdiction foreign to our constitution, and unacknowledged by our laws; giving his Assent to their Acts of pretended Legislation:

For Quartering large bodies of armed troops among us:

For protecting them, by a mock Trial, from punishment for any Murders which they should commit on the Inhabitants of these States:

For cutting off our Trade with all parts of the world:

For imposing Taxes on us without our Consent:

For depriving us in many cases, of the benefits of Trial by Jury:

For transporting us beyond Seas to be tried for pretended offences

For abolishing the free System of English Laws in a neighbouring Province, establishing therein an Arbitrary government, and enlarging its Boundaries so as to render it at once an example and fit instrument for introducing the same absolute rule into these Colonies:

For taking away our Charters, abolishing our most valuable Laws, and altering fundamentally the Forms of our Governments:

For suspending our own Legislatures, and declaring themselves invested with power to legislate for us in all cases whatsoever.

He has abdicated Government here, by declaring us out of his Protection and waging War against us.

He has plundered our seas, ravaged our Coasts, burnt our towns, and destroyed the lives of our people.

He is at this time transporting large Armies of foreign Mercenaries to compleat the works of death, desolation and tyranny, already begun with circumstances of Cruelty & perfidy scarcely paralleled in the most barbarous ages, and totally unworthy the Head of a civilized nation.

He has constrained our fellow Citizens taken Captive on the high Seas to bear Arms against their Country, to become the executioners of their friends and Brethren, or to fall themselves by their Hands.

He has excited domestic insurrections amongst us, and has endeavoured to bring on the inhabitants of our frontiers, the merciless Indian Savages, whose known rule of warfare, is an undistinguished destruction of all ages, sexes and conditions.

In every stage of these Oppressions We have Petitioned for Redress in the most humble terms: Our repeated Petitions have been answered only by repeated injury. A Prince whose character is thus marked by every act which may define a Tyrant, is unfit to be the ruler of a free people.

Nor have We been wanting in attentions to our Brittish brethren. We have warned them from time to time of attempts by their legislature to extend an unwarrantable jurisdiction over us. We have reminded them of the circumstances of our emigration and settlement here. We have appealed to their native justice and magnanimity, and we have conjured them by the ties of our common kindred to disavow these usurpations, which, would inevitably interrupt our connections and correspondence. They too have been deaf to the voice of justice and of consanguinity. We must, therefore, acquiesce in the necessity, which denounces our

Separation, and hold them, as we hold the rest of mankind, Enemies in War, in Peace Friends.

We, therefore, the Representatives of the united States of America, in General Congress, Assembled, appealing to the Supreme Judge of the world for the rectitude of our intentions, do, in the Name, and by Authority of the good People of these Colonies, solemnly publish and declare, That these United Colonies are, and of Right ought to be Free and Independent States; that they are Absolved from all Allegiance to the British Crown, and that all political connection between them and the State of Great Britain, is and ought to be totally dissolved; and that as Free and Independent States, they have full Power to levy War, conclude Peace, contract Alliances, establish Commerce, and to do all other Acts and Things which Independent States may of right do. And for the support of this Declaration, with a firm reliance on the protection of divine Providence, we mutually pledge to each other our Lives, our Fortunes and our sacred Honor.

Signed by ORDER and in BEHALF of the CONGRESS,

JOHN HANCOCK, PRESIDENT.

ATTEST.
CHARLES THOMSON, SECRETARY

DELAWARE
George Read
Caesar Rodney
Thomas McKean
PENNSYLVANIA
George Clymer
Benjamin Franklin
Robert Morris
John Morton
Benjamin Rush
George Ross
James Smith
James Wilson
George Taylor
MASSACHUSETTS
John Adams
Samuel Adams
John Hancock
Robert Treat Paine
Elbridge Gerry
NEW HAMPSHIRE
Josiah Bartlett
William Whipple
Matthew Thornton
RHODE ISLAND
Stephen Hopkins
William Ellery
NEW YORK
Lewis Morris
Philip Livingston
Francis Lewis
William Floyd

GEORGIA
Button Gwinnett
Lyman Hall
George Walton
VIRGINIA
Richard Henry Lee
Francis Lightfoot Lee
Carter Braxton
Benjamin Harrison
Thomas Jefferson
George Wythe
Thomas Nelson, Jr.
NORTH CAROLINA
William Hooper
John Penn
Joseph Hewes
SOUTH CAROLINA
Edward Rutledge
Arthur Middleton
Thomas Lynch, Jr.
Thomas Heyward, Jr.

NEW JERSEY
Abraham Clark
John Hart
Francis Hopkinson
Richard Stockton
John Witherspoon
CONNECTICUT
Samuel Huntington
Roger Sherman
William Williams
Oliver Wolcott
MARYLAND
Charles Carroll
Samuel Chase
Thomas Stone
William Pacd

Author's Summary:
The Declaration of Independence

IN 1776, THE DECLARATION OF INDEPENDENCE opens with a preamble explaining why the Colonies have overthrown their unjust ruler and have chosen to take their own place, as a separate nation in the world.

The Declaration further states that: "All men are created equal" and "There are certain unalienable rights" that governments should never violate, and "That these rights include the right to life, liberty and the pursuit of happiness" it is because:

When a government fails to protect those promised rights, it is not only the responsibility, but also the duty of the people to overthrow that government and in its place establish a government that is designed to once again protect those rights of the people.

The lesson here is since ruling powers should not be overthrown for trivial reasons. In this particular case, the Founders list the long history of abuses that led the Colonists to overthrow England, their tyrannical ruler.

In 1781, many men in the Second Continental Congress wrote the *Articles of Confederation* which loosely outlined how this new nation might agree to certain principals of association and continuous harmony.

After their writing of *The Federalist* in 1787, Alexander Hamilton, James Madison and John Jay supported, proposed, and earnestly urged the Continental Congress to create a succinct Constitution for this new country.

In 1788, with Thomas Jefferson away in France, John Adams in England James Madison and Alexander Hamilton undertook framing first draft of the first Constitution.

In 1789 the Continental Congress, with drama and disagreement, ratified the final *United States Constitution*.

So, it wasn't easy for our founders. The United States of America came together with many minds, over many years.

Hang in there! I've added even more pages for your education. Next you'll have an opportunity to review our Constitution followed by its *Bill of Rights*.

Then come a number of great writings and sound ideas from some of our most patriotic Americans.

Please, read the following magnificent words very slowly.

Think about how protected you are by these words and realize why you need to cooperate, or dissent, with the representatives of your state and federal government.

If you don't act, your basic *constitutionally guaranteed* freedoms will slowly be taken from you.

CHAPTER THREE

The United States Constitution

Note: The following text is a transcription of the Constitution as it was inscribed by Jacob Shallus on parchment (the document on display in the Rotunda at the National Archives Museum.) The spelling and punctuation reflect the
original. Italics denote sections affected by subsequent amendments.

We the People of the United States, in Order to form a more perfect
Union, establish Justice, insure domestic Tranquility, provide for the
common defence, promote the general Welfare, and secure the Blessings
of Liberty to ourselves and our Posterity, do ordain and establish this
Constitution for the United States of America.

Article. I.

SECTION. 1.
All legislative Powers herein granted shall be vested in a Congress
of the United States, which shall consist of a Senate and House of
Representatives.

SECTION. 2.
The House of Representatives shall be composed of Members chosen
every second Year by the People of the several States, and the Electors
in each State shall have the Qualifications requisite for Electors of the
most numerous Branch of the State Legislature.

No Person shall be a Representative who shall not have attained to the
Age of twenty five Years, and been seven Years a Citizen of the United
States, and who shall not, when elected, be an Inhabitant of that State in
which he shall be chosen.

*Representatives and direct Taxes shall be apportioned among the several
States which may be included within this Union, according to their respective
Numbers, which shall be determined by adding to the whole Number of free
Persons, including those bound to Service for a Term of Years, and excluding
Indians not taxed, three fifths of all other Persons. The actual Enumeration*

shall be made within three Years after the first Meeting of the Congress of the United States, and within every subsequent Term of ten Years, in such Manner as they shall by Law direct. The Number of Representatives shall not exceed one for every thirty Thousand, but each State shall have at Least one Representative; and until such enumeration shall be made, the State of New Hampshire shall be entitled to chuse three, Massachusetts eight, Rhode-Island and Providence Plantations one, Connecticut five, New-York six, New Jersey four, Pennsylvania eight, Delaware one, Maryland six, Virginia ten, North Carolina five, South Carolina five, and Georgia three.

When vacancies happen in the Representation from any State, the Executive Authority thereof shall issue Writs of Election to fill such Vacancies.

The House of Representatives shall chuse their Speaker and other Officers; and shall have the sole Power of Impeachment.

SECTION. 3.
The Senate of the United States shall be composed of two Senators from each State, chosen by the Legislature thereof, for six Years; and each Senator shall have one Vote.

Immediately after they shall be assembled in Consequence of the first Election, they shall be divided as equally as may be into three Classes. The Seats of the Senators of the first Class shall be vacated at the Expiration of the second Year, of the second Class at the Expiration of the fourth Year, and of the third Class at the Expiration of the sixth Year, so that one third may be chosen every second Year; and if Vacancies happen by Resignation, or otherwise, during the Recess of the Legislature of any State, the Executive thereof may make temporary Appointments until the next Meeting of the Legislature, which shall then fill such Vacancies.

No Person shall be a Senator who shall not have attained to the Age of thirty Years, and been nine Years a Citizen of the United States, and who shall not, when elected, be an Inhabitant of that State for which he shall be chosen.

The Vice President of the United States shall be President of the Senate, but shall have no Vote, unless they be equally divided.

The Senate shall chuse their other Officers, and also a President pro tempore, in the Absence of the Vice President, or when he shall exercise the Office of President of the United States.

The Senate shall have the sole Power to try all Impeachments. When sitting for that Purpose, they shall be on Oath or Affirmation. When the President of the United States is tried, the Chief Justice shall preside: And no Person shall be convicted without the Concurrence of two thirds of the Members present.

Judgment in Cases of Impeachment shall not extend further than to removal from Office, and disqualification to hold and enjoy any Office of honor, Trust or Profit under the United States: but the Party convicted shall nevertheless be liable and subject to Indictment, Trial, Judgment and Punishment, according to Law.

SECTION. 4.

The Times, Places and Manner of holding Elections for Senators and Representatives, shall be prescribed in each State by the Legislature thereof; but the Congress may at any time by Law make or alter such Regulations, except as to the Places of chusing Senators.

The Congress shall assemble at least once in every Year, and such Meeting shall be on *the first Monday in December, unless they shall by Law appoint a different Day.*

SECTION. 5.

Each House shall be the Judge of the Elections, Returns and Qualifications of its own Members, and a Majority of each shall constitute a Quorum to do Business; but a smaller Number may adjourn from day to day, and may be authorized to compel the Attendance of absent Members, in such Manner, and under such Penalties as each House may provide.

Each House may determine the Rules of its Proceedings, punish its Members for disorderly Behaviour, and, with the Concurrence of two thirds, expel a Member.

Each House shall keep a Journal of its Proceedings, and from time to time publish the same, excepting such Parts as may in their Judgment require Secrecy; and the Yeas and Nays of the Members of either House on any question shall, at the Desire of one fifth of those Present, be entered on the Journal.

Neither House, during the Session of Congress, shall, without the Consent of the other, adjourn for more than three days, nor to any other Place than that in which the two Houses shall be sitting.

SECTION. 6.

The Senators and Representatives shall receive a Compensation for their Services, to be ascertained by Law, and paid out of the Treasury of the United States. They shall in all Cases, except Treason, Felony and Breach of the Peace, be privileged from Arrest during their Attendance at the Session of their respective Houses, and in going to and returning from the same; and for any Speech or Debate in either House, they shall not be questioned in any other Place.

No Senator or Representative shall, during the Time for which he was elected, be appointed to any civil Office under the Authority of the United States, which shall have been created, or the Emoluments whereof shall have been encreased during such time; and no Person holding any Office under the United States, shall be a Member of either House during his Continuance in Office.

SECTION. 7.

All Bills for raising Revenue shall originate in the House of Representatives; but the Senate may propose or concur with Amendments as on other Bills.

Every Bill which shall have passed the House of Representatives and the Senate, shall, before it become a Law, be presented to the President of the United States; If he approve he shall sign it, but if not he shall return it, with his Objections to that House in which it shall have originated, who shall enter the Objections at large on their Journal, and proceed to reconsider it. If after such Reconsideration two thirds of that House shall agree to pass the Bill, it shall be sent, together with the Objections, to the other House, by which it shall likewise be reconsidered, and if approved by two thirds of that House, it shall become a Law. But in all such Cases the Votes of both Houses shall be determined by yeas and Nays, and the Names of the Persons voting for and against the Bill shall be entered on the Journal of each House respectively. If any Bill shall not be returned by the President within ten Days (Sundays excepted) after it shall have been presented to him, the Same shall be a Law, in like Manner as if he had signed it, unless the Congress by their Adjournment prevent its Return, in which Case it shall not be a Law.

Every Order, Resolution, or Vote to which the Concurrence of the Senate and House of Representatives may be necessary (except on a question of Adjournment) shall be presented to the President of the United States; and before the Same shall take Effect, shall be approved by him, or being disapproved by him, shall be repassed by two thirds of the Senate and House of Representatives, according to the Rules and Limitations prescribed in the Case of a Bill.

SECTION. 8.
The Congress shall have Power To lay and collect Taxes, Duties, Imposts and Excises, to pay the Debts and provide for the common Defence and general Welfare of the United States; but all Duties, Imposts and Excises shall be uniform throughout the United States;

To borrow Money on the credit of the United States;

To regulate Commerce with foreign Nations, and among the several States, and with the Indian Tribes;

To establish an uniform Rule of Naturalization, and uniform Laws on the subject of Bankruptcies throughout the United States;

To coin Money, regulate the Value thereof, and of foreign Coin, and fix the Standard of Weights and Measures;

To provide for the Punishment of counterfeiting the Securities and current Coin of the United States;

To establish Post Offices and post Roads;

To promote the Progress of Science and useful Arts, by securing for limited Times to Authors and Inventors the exclusive Right to their respective Writings and Discoveries;

To constitute Tribunals inferior to the supreme Court;

To define and punish Piracies and Felonies committed on the high Seas, and Offences against the Law of Nations;

To declare War, grant Letters of Marque and Reprisal, and make Rules concerning Captures on Land and Water;

To raise and support Armies, but no Appropriation of Money to that Use shall be for a longer Term than two Years;

To provide and maintain a Navy;

To make Rules for the Government and Regulation of the land and naval Forces;

To provide for calling forth the Militia to execute the Laws of the Union, suppress Insurrections and repel Invasions;

To provide for organizing, arming, and disciplining, the Militia, and for governing such Part of them as may be employed in the Service of the United States, reserving to the States respectively, the Appointment of the Officers, and the Authority of training the Militia according to the discipline prescribed by Congress;

To exercise exclusive Legislation in all Cases whatsoever, over such District (not exceeding ten Miles square) as may, by Cession of particular States, and the Acceptance of Congress, become the Seat of the Government of the United States, and to exercise like Authority over all Places purchased by the Consent of the Legislature of the State in which the Same shall be, for the Erection of Forts, Magazines, Arsenals, dock-Yards, and other needful Buildings;—And

To make all Laws which shall be necessary and proper for carrying into Execution the foregoing Powers, and all other Powers vested by this Constitution in the Government of the United States, or in any Department or Officer thereof.

SECTION. 9.

The Migration or Importation of such Persons as any of the States now existing shall think proper to admit, shall not be prohibited by the

Congress prior to the Year one thousand eight hundred and eight, but a Tax or duty may be imposed on such Importation, not exceeding ten dollars for each Person.

The Privilege of the Writ of Habeas Corpus shall not be suspended, unless when in Cases of Rebellion or Invasion the public Safety may require it.

No Bill of Attainder or ex post facto Law shall be passed.

No Capitation, or other direct, Tax shall be laid, *unless in Proportion to the Census or enumeration herein before directed to be taken.*

No Tax or Duty shall be laid on Articles exported from any State.

No Preference shall be given by any Regulation of Commerce or Revenue to the Ports of one State over those of another: nor shall Vessels bound to, or from, one State, be obliged to enter, clear, or pay Duties in another.

No Money shall be drawn from the Treasury, but in Consequence of Appropriations made by Law; and a regular Statement and Account of the Receipts and Expenditures of all public Money shall be published from time to time.

No Title of Nobility shall be granted by the United States: And no Person holding any Office of Profit or Trust under them, shall, without the Consent of the Congress, accept of any present, Emolument, Office, or Title, of any kind whatever, from any King, Prince, or foreign State.

SECTION. 10.
No State shall enter into any Treaty, Alliance, or Confederation; grant Letters of Marque and Reprisal; coin Money; emit Bills of Credit; make any Thing but gold and silver Coin a Tender in Payment of Debts; pass any Bill of Attainder, ex post facto Law, or Law impairing the Obligation of Contracts, or grant any Title of Nobility.

No State shall, without the Consent of the Congress, lay any Imposts or Duties on Imports or Exports, except what may be absolutely necessary for executing it's inspection Laws: and the net Produce of all Duties and Imposts, laid by any State on Imports or Exports, shall be for the Use of the Treasury of the United States; and all such Laws shall be subject to the Revision and Controul of the Congress.

No State shall, without the Consent of Congress, lay any Duty of Tonnage, keep Troops, or Ships of War in time of Peace, enter into any Agreement or Compact with another State, or with a foreign Power, or engage in War, unless actually invaded, or in such imminent Danger as will not admit of delay.

Article. II.

SECTION. 1.

The executive Power shall be vested in a President of the United States of America. He shall hold his Office during the Term of four Years, and, together with the Vice President, chosen for the same Term, be elected, as follows

Each State shall appoint, in such Manner as the Legislature thereof may direct, a Number of Electors, equal to the whole Number of Senators and Representatives to which the State may be entitled in the Congress: but no Senator or Representative, or Person holding an Office of Trust or Profit under the United States, shall be appointed an Elector.

The Electors shall meet in their respective States, and vote by Ballot for two Persons, of whom one at least shall not be an Inhabitant of the same State with themselves. And they shall make a List of all the Persons voted for, and of the Number of Votes for each; which List they shall sign and certify, and transmit sealed to the Seat of the Government of the United States, directed to the President of the Senate. The President of the Senate shall, in the Presence of the Senate and House of Representatives, open all the Certificates, and the Votes shall then be counted. The Person having the greatest Number of Votes shall be the President, if such Number be a Majority of the whole Number of Electors appointed; and if there be more than one who have such Majority, and have an equal Number of Votes, then the House of Representatives shall immediately chuse by Ballot one of them for President; and if no Person have a Majority, then from the five highest on the List the said House shall in like Manner chuse the President. But in chusing the President, the Votes shall be taken by States, the Representation from each State having one Vote; A quorum for this Purpose shall consist of a Member or Members from two thirds of the States, and a Majority of all the States shall be necessary to a Choice. In every Case, after the Choice of the President, the Person having the greatest Number of Votes of the Electors shall be the Vice President. But if there should remain two or more who have equal Votes, the Senate shall chuse from them by Ballot the Vice President.

The Congress may determine the Time of chusing the Electors, and the Day on which they shall give their Votes; which Day shall be the same throughout the United States.

No Person except a natural born Citizen, or a Citizen of the United States, at the time of the Adoption of this Constitution, shall be eligible to the Office of President; neither shall any Person be eligible to that Office who shall not have attained to the Age of thirty five Years, and been fourteen Years a Resident within the United States.

In Case of the Removal of the President from Office, or of his Death, Resignation, or Inability to discharge the Powers and Duties of the said Office, the Same shall devolve on the Vice President, and the Congress may by Law provide for the Case of Removal, Death, Resignation or Inability, both of the President and Vice President, declaring what Officer shall then act as President, and such Officer shall act accordingly, until the Disability be removed, or a President shall be elected.

The President shall, at stated Times, receive for his Services, a Compensation, which shall neither be encreased nor diminished during the Period for which he shall have been elected, and he shall not receive within that Period any other Emolument from the United States, or any of them.

Before he enter on the Execution of his Office, he shall take the following Oath or Affirmation:—"I do solemnly swear (or affirm) that I will faithfully execute the Office of President of the United States, and will to the best of my Ability, preserve, protect and defend the Constitution of the United States."

SECTION. 2.
The President shall be Commander in Chief of the Army and Navy of the United States, and of the Militia of the several States, when called into the actual Service of the United States; he may require the Opinion, in writing, of the principal Officer in each of the executive Departments,

upon any Subject relating to the Duties of their respective Offices, and he shall have Power to grant Reprieves and Pardons for Offences against the United States, except in Cases of Impeachment.

He shall have Power, by and with the Advice and Consent of the Senate, to make Treaties, provided two thirds of the Senators present concur; and he shall nominate, and by and with the Advice and Consent of the Senate, shall appoint Ambassadors, other public Ministers and Consuls, Judges of the supreme Court, and all other Officers of the United States, whose Appointments are not herein otherwise provided for, and which shall be established by Law: but the Congress may by Law vest the Appointment of such inferior Officers, as they think proper, in the President alone, in the Courts of Law, or in the Heads of Departments.

The President shall have Power to fill up all Vacancies that may happen during the Recess of the Senate, by granting Commissions which shall expire at the End of their next Session.

SECTION. 3.
He shall from time to time give to the Congress Information of the State of the Union, and recommend to their Consideration such Measures as he shall judge necessary and expedient; he may, on extraordinary Occasions, convene both Houses, or either of them, and in Case of Disagreement between them, with Respect to the Time of Adjournment, he may adjourn them to such Time as he shall think proper; he shall receive Ambassadors and other public Ministers; he shall take Care that the Laws be faithfully executed, and shall Commission all the Officers of the United States.

SECTION. 4.
The President, Vice President and all civil Officers of the United States, shall be removed from Office on Impeachment for, and Conviction of, Treason, Bribery, or other high Crimes and Misdemeanors.

Article III.

SECTION. 1.
The judicial Power of the United States, shall be vested in one supreme Court, and in such inferior Courts as the Congress may from time to time ordain and establish. The Judges, both of the supreme and inferior Courts, shall hold their Offices during good Behaviour, and shall,

at stated Times, receive for their Services, a Compensation, which shall not be diminished during their Continuance in Office.

SECTION. 2.

The judicial Power shall extend to all Cases, in Law and Equity, arising under this Constitution, the Laws of the United States, and Treaties made, or which shall be made, under their Authority;—to all Cases affecting Ambassadors, other public Ministers and Consuls;—to all Cases of admiralty and maritime Jurisdiction;—to Controversies to which the United States shall be a Party;—to Controversies between two or more States;— between a State and Citizens of another State,—between Citizens of different States,—between Citizens of the same State claiming Lands under Grants of different States, and between a State, or the Citizens thereof, and foreign States, Citizens or Subjects.

In all Cases affecting Ambassadors, other public Ministers and Consuls, and those in which a State shall be Party, the supreme Court shall have original Jurisdiction. In all the other Cases before mentioned, the supreme Court shall have appellate Jurisdiction, both as to Law and Fact, with such Exceptions, and under such Regulations as the Congress shall make.

The Trial of all Crimes, except in Cases of Impeachment, shall be by Jury; and such Trial shall be held in the State where the said Crimes shall have been committed; but when not committed within any State, the Trial shall be at such Place or Places as the Congress may by Law have directed.

SECTION. 3.

Treason against the United States, shall consist only in levying War against them, or in adhering to their Enemies, giving them Aid and Comfort. No Person shall be convicted of Treason unless on the Testimony of two Witnesses to the same overt Act, or on Confession in open Court.

The Congress shall have Power to declare the Punishment of Treason, but no Attainder of Treason shall work Corruption of Blood, or Forfeiture except during the Life of the Person attainted.

Article. IV.

SECTION. 1.

Full Faith and Credit shall be given in each State to the public Acts, Records, and judicial Proceedings of every other State. And the Congress may by general Laws prescribe the Manner in which such Acts, Records and Proceedings shall be proved, and the Effect thereof.

SECTION. 2.

The Citizens of each State shall be entitled to all Privileges and Immunities of Citizens in the several States.

A Person charged in any State with Treason, Felony, or other Crime, who shall flee from Justice, and be found in another State, shall on Demand of the executive Authority of the State from which he fled, be delivered up, to be removed to the State having Jurisdiction of the Crime.

No Person held to Service or Labour in one State, under the Laws thereof, escaping into another, shall, in Consequence of any Law or Regulation therein, be discharged from such Service or Labour, but shall be delivered up on Claim of the Party to whom such Service or Labour may be due.

SECTION. 3.

New States may be admitted by the Congress into this Union; but no new State shall be formed or erected within the Jurisdiction of any other State; nor any State be formed by the Junction of two or more States, or Parts of States, without the Consent of the Legislatures of the States concerned as well as of the Congress.

The Congress shall have Power to dispose of and make all needful Rules and Regulations respecting the Territory or other Property belonging to the United States; and nothing in this Constitution shall be so construed as to Prejudice any Claims of the United States, or of any particular State.

SECTION. 4.

The United States shall guarantee to every State in this Union a Republican Form of Government, and shall protect each of them against Invasion; and on Application of the Legislature, or of the Executive (when the Legislature cannot be convened), against domestic Violence.

Article. V.

The Congress, whenever two thirds of both Houses shall deem it necessary, shall propose Amendments to this Constitution, or, on the Application of the Legislatures of two thirds of the several States, shall call a Convention for proposing Amendments, which, in either Case, shall be valid to all Intents and Purposes, as Part of this Constitution, when ratified by the Legislatures of three fourths of the several States, or by Conventions in three fourths thereof, as the one or the other Mode of Ratification may be proposed by the Congress; Provided that no Amendment which may be made prior to the Year One thousand eight hundred and eight shall in any Manner affect the first and fourth Clauses in the Ninth Section of the first Article; and that no State, without its Consent, shall be deprived of its equal Suffrage in the Senate.

Article. VI.

All Debts contracted and Engagements entered into, before the Adoption of this Constitution, shall be as valid against the United States under this Constitution, as under the Confederation.

This Constitution, and the Laws of the United States which shall be made in Pursuance thereof; and all Treaties made, or which shall be made, under the Authority of the United States, shall be the supreme Law of the Land; and the Judges in every State shall be bound thereby, any Thing in the Constitution or Laws of any State to the Contrary notwithstanding.

The Senators and Representatives before mentioned, and the Members of the several State Legislatures, and all executive and judicial Officers, both of the United States and of the several States, shall be bound by Oath or Affirmation, to support this Constitution; but no religious Test shall ever be required as a Qualification to any Office or public Trust under the United States.

Article. VII.

The Ratification of the Conventions of nine States, shall be sufficient for the Establishment of this Constitution between the States so ratifying the Same.

The Word, "the," being interlined between the seventh and eighth Lines of the first Page, The Word "Thirty" being partly written on an Erazure

in the fifteenth Line of the first Page, The Words "is tried" being interlined between the thirty second and thirty third Lines of the first Page
and the Word "the" being interlined between the forty third and forty
fourth Lines of the second Page.
Attest William Jackson Secretary

done in Convention by the Unanimous Consent of the States present
the Seventeenth Day of September in the Year of our Lord one thousand
seven hundred and Eighty seven and of the Independance of the United
States of America the Twelfth In witness whereof We have hereunto
subscribed our Names,

G°. Washington
Presidt and deputy from Virginia

DELAWARE
Geo: Read
Gunning Bedford jun
John Dickinson
Richard Bassett
Jaco: Broom

MARYLAND
James McHenry
Dan of St Thos. Jenifer
Danl. Carroll

VIRGINIA
John Blair
James Madison Jr.

NORTH CAROLINA
Wm. Blount
Richd. Dobbs Spaight
Hu Williamson

SOUTH CAROLINA
J. Rutledge
Charles Cotesworth Pinckney
Charles Pinckney
Pierce Butler

GEORGIA
William Few
Abr Baldwin

NEW HAMPSHIRE
John Langdon
Nicholas Gilman

MASSACHUSETTS
Nathaniel Gorham
Rufus King

CONNECTICUT
Wm. Saml. Johnson
Roger Sherman

NEW YORK
Alexander Hamilton

NEW JERSEY
Wil: Livingston
David Brearley
Wm. Paterson
Jona: Dayton

PENNSYLVANIA
B Franklin
Thomas Mifflin
Robt. Morris
Geo. Clymer
Thos. FitzSimons
Jared Ingersoll
James Wilson
Gouv Morris

Author's summary of the US Constitution

AND, WHAT DO THESE WORDS actually mean?

This Constitution defines the fundamental structure and laws of the United States, setting forth the three principal branches of our government:

- •Executive

- •Legislative

- •Judicial

It further outlines the jurisdictions and powers of these branches, clearly propounding the basic rights of all U.S. citizens.

The essential principle of this amazing document is that our government must adhere to the rule of law within a defined system of checks and balances. For the government to operate fairly, the people must never allow these three branches to be combined. Operating as one body, with one voice controlling all decisions made, would result in an authoritarian and oppressive government; ultimately, a dictatorship.

If we should allow that to happen, liberty and freedom will perish and be lost forever.

But you must be honored. We have the oldest written and continuing national statutes in the modern world. The Constitution of the United States of America has become a landmark legal document in Western civilization.

CHAPTER FOUR

The Bill of Rights and Subsequent Amendments

Amendments 1-10 of the Constitution.

The Conventions of a number of the States having, at the time of adopting the Constitution, expressed a desire, in order to prevent misconstruction or abuse of its powers, that further declaratory and restrictive clauses should be added, and as extending the ground of public confidence in the Government will best insure the beneficent ends of its institution;

Resolved, by the Senate and House of Representatives of the United States of America, in Congress assembled, two-thirds of both Houses concurring, that the following articles be proposed to the Legislatures of the several States, as amendments to the Constitution of the United States; all or any of which articles, when ratified by three-fourths of the said Legislatures, to be valid to all intents and purposes as part of the said Constitution, namely:

Amendment I

Congress shall make no law respecting an establishment of religion, or prohibiting the free exercise thereof; or abridging the freedom of speech, or of the press; or the right of the people peaceably to assemble, and to petition the government for a redress of grievances.

Amendment II

A well regulated militia, being necessary to the security of a free state, the right of the people to keep and bear arms, shall not be infringed.

Amendment III

No soldier shall, in time of peace be quartered in any house, without the consent of the owner, nor in time of war, but in a manner to be prescribed by law.

Amendment IV

The right of the people to be secure in their persons, houses, pa-
pers, and effects, against unreasonable searches and seizures, shall not
be violated, and no warrants shall issue, but upon probable cause, supported by oath or affirmation, and particularly describing the place to be
searched, and the persons or things to be seized.

Amendment V

No person shall be held to answer for a capital, or otherwise infamous crime, unless on a presentment or indictment of a grand jury, except in cases arising in the land or naval forces, or in the militia, when
in actual service in time of war or public danger; nor shall any person be
subject for the same offense to be twice put in jeopardy of life or limb;
nor shall be compelled in any criminal case to be a witness against himself, nor be deprived of life, liberty, or property, without due process
of law; nor shall private property be taken for public use, without just
compensation.

Amendment VI

In all criminal prosecutions, the accused shall enjoy the right to a
speedy and public trial, by an impartial jury of the state and district
wherein the crime shall have been committed, which district shall have
been previously ascertained by law, and to be informed of the nature
and cause of the accusation; to be confronted with the witnesses against
him; to have compulsory process for obtaining witnesses in his favor,
and to have the assistance of counsel for his defense.

Amendment VII

In suits at common law, where the value in controversy shall exceed
twenty dollars, the right of trial by jury shall be preserved, and no fact
tried by a jury, shall be otherwise reexamined in any court of the United
States, than according to the rules of the common law.

Amendment VIII

Excessive bail shall not be required, nor excessive fines imposed, nor
cruel and unusual punishments inflicted.

Amendment IX

The enumeration in the Constitution, of certain rights, shall not be construed to deny or disparage others retained by the people.

Amendment X

The powers not delegated to the United States by the Constitution, nor prohibited by it to the states, are reserved to the states respectively, or to the people.

Amendment XI

Passed by Congress March 4, 1794. Ratified February 7, 1795.

Note: Article III, section 2, of the Constitution was modified by amendment 11.

The Judicial power of the United States shall not be construed to extend to any suit in law or equity, commenced or prosecuted against one of the United States by Citizens of another State, or by Citizens or Subjects of any Foreign State.

Amendment XII

Passed by Congress December 9, 1803. Ratified June 15, 1804.

Note: A portion of Article II, section 1 of the Constitution was superseded by the 12th amendment.

The Electors shall meet in their respective states and vote by ballot for President and Vice-President, one of whom, at least, shall not be an inhabitant of the same state with themselves; they shall name in their ballots the person voted for as President, and in distinct ballots the person voted for as Vice-President, and they shall make distinct lists of all persons voted for as President, and of all persons voted for as Vice-President, and of the number of votes for each, which lists they shall sign and certify, and transmit sealed to the seat of the government of the United States, directed to the President of the Senate; -- the President of the Senate shall, in the presence of the Senate and House of Representatives, open all the certificates and the votes shall then be counted; -- The person having the greatest number of votes for President, shall be the President, if such number be a majority of the whole number of Electors appointed; and if no person have such majority, then from the persons having the highest numbers not exceeding three on the list of those voted for as President, the House of Representatives shall choose immediately, by ballot, the President. But in choosing the President, the votes shall be taken by states, the representation from each state having one vote; a quorum for this purpose shall consist of a member or members from two-thirds of the states, and a majority of all the states shall be necessary to a choice. [And if the House of Representatives shall not choose a President whenever the right of choice shall devolve upon them, before the fourth day of March next following, then the Vice-President shall act as President, as in case of the death or other constitutional disability of the

President. The person having the greatest number of votes as Vice-President, shall be the Vice-President, if such number be a majority of the whole number of Electors appointed, and if no person have a majority, then from the two highest numbers on the list, the *Senate* shall choose the Vice-President; a quorum for the purpose shall consist of two-thirds of the whole number of Senators, and a majority of the whole number shall be necessary to a choice. But no person constitutionally ineligible to the office of President shall be eligible to that of Vice-President of the United States.

Superseded by section 3 of the 20th amendment.

Amendment XIII

Passed by Congress January 31, 1865. Ratified December 6, 1865.
Note: A portion of Article IV, section 2, of the Constitution was superseded by the 13th amendment.

SECTION 1.
Neither slavery nor involuntary servitude, except as a punishment for crime whereof the party shall have been duly convicted, shall exist within the United States, or any place subject to their jurisdiction.

SECTION 2.
Congress shall have power to enforce this article by appropriate legislation.

Amendment XIV

Passed by Congress June 13, 1866. Ratified July 9, 1868.
Note: Article I, section 2, of the Constitution was modified by section 2 of the 14th amendment.

SECTION 1.
All persons born or naturalized in the United States, and subject to the jurisdiction thereof, are citizens of the United States and of the State

wherein they reside. No State shall make or enforce any law which shall abridge the privileges or immunities of citizens of the United States; nor shall any State deprive any person of life, liberty, or property, without due process of law; nor deny to any person within its jurisdiction the equal protection of the laws.

SECTION 2.

Representatives shall be apportioned among the several States according to their respective numbers, counting the whole number of persons in each State, excluding Indians not taxed. But when the right to

vote at any election for the choice of electors for President and Vice-President of the United States, Representatives in Congress, the Executive and Judicial officers of a State, or the members of the Legislature thereof, is denied to any of the male inhabitants of such State, being twenty-one years of age,* and citizens of the United States,

or in any way abridged, except for participation in rebellion, or other crime, the basis of representation therein shall be reduced in the proportion which the number of such male citizens shall bear to the whole number of male citizens twenty-one years of age in such State.

SECTION 3.

No person shall be a Senator or Representative in Congress, or elector of President and Vice-President, or hold any office, civil or military, under the United States, or under any State, who, having previously taken an oath, as a member of Congress, or as an officer of the United States, or as a member of any State legislature, or as an executive or judicial officer of any State, to support the Constitution of the United States, shall have engaged in insurrection or rebellion against the same, or given aid or comfort to the enemies thereof. But Congress may by a vote of two-thirds of each House, remove such disability.

SECTION 4.

The validity of the public debt of the United States, authorized by law, including debts incurred for payment of pensions and bounties for services in suppressing insurrection or rebellion, shall not be questioned. But neither the United States nor any State shall assume or pay any debt or obligation incurred in aid of insurrection or rebellion against the United States, or any claim for the loss or emancipation of any slave; but all such debts, obligations and claims shall be held illegal and void.

SECTION 5.

The Congress shall have the power to enforce, by appropriate legislation, the provisions of this article.

Changed by section 1 of the 26th amendment.

Amendment XV

Passed by Congress February 26, 1869. Ratified February 3, 1870.

SECTION 1.

The right of citizens of the United States to vote shall not be denied or abridged by the United States or by any State on account of race, color, or previous condition of servitude.

SECTION 2.

The Congress shall have the power to enforce this article by appropriate legislation.

Amendment XVI

Passed by Congress July 2, 1909. Ratified February 3, 1913.

Note: Article I, section 9, of the Constitution was modified by amendment 16.

The Congress shall have power to lay and collect taxes on incomes, from whatever source derived, without apportionment among the several States, and without regard to any census or enumeration.

Amendment XVII

Passed by Congress May 13, 1912. Ratified April 8, 1913.

Note: Article I, section 3, of the Constitution was modified by the 17th amendment.

The Senate of the United States shall be composed of two Senators from each State, elected by the people thereof, for six years; and each Senator shall have one vote. The electors in each State shall have the qualifications requisite for electors of the most numerous branch of the State legislatures. When vacancies happen in the representation of any State in the Senate, the executive authority of such State shall issue writs of election to fill such vacancies: Provided, That the legislature of any State may empower the executive thereof to make temporary appointments until the people fill the vacancies by election as the legislature may direct. This amendment shall not be so construed as to affect the election or term of any Senator chosen before it becomes valid as part of the Constitution.

Amendment XVIII

Passed by Congress December 18, 1917. Ratified January 16, 1919. Repealed by amendment 21.

SECTION 1.

After one year from the ratification of this article the manufacture, sale, or transportation of intoxicating liquors within, the importation thereof into, or the exportation thereof from the United States and all territory subject to the jurisdiction thereof for beverage purposes is hereby prohibited.

SECTION 2.

The Congress and the several States shall have concurrent power to enforce this article by appropriate legislation.

SECTION 3.

This article shall be inoperative unless it shall have been ratified as an amendment to the Constitution by the legislatures of the several States, as provided in the Constitution, within seven years from the date of the submission hereof to the States by the Congress.

Amendment XIX

Passed by Congress June 4, 1919. Ratified August 18, 1920.

The right of citizens of the United States to vote shall not be denied or abridged by the United States or by any State on account of sex. Congress shall have power to enforce this article by appropriate legislation.

Amendment XX

Passed by Congress March 2, 1932. Ratified January 23, 1933.
Note: Article I, section 4, of the Constitution was modified by section 2 of this amendment. In addition, a portion of the 12th amendment was superseded by section 3.

SECTION 1.

The terms of the President and the Vice President shall end at noon on the 20th day of January, and the terms of Senators and Representatives at noon on the 3d day of January, of the years in which such terms would have ended if this article had not been ratified; and the terms of their successors shall then begin.

SECTION 2.

The Congress shall assemble at least once in every year, and such meeting shall begin at noon on the 3d day of January, unless they shall by law appoint a different day.

SECTION 3.

If, at the time fixed for the beginning of the term of the President, the President elect shall have died, the Vice President elect shall become President. If a President shall not have been chosen before the time fixed for the beginning of his term, or if the President elect shall have failed to qualify, then the Vice President elect shall act as President until a President shall have qualified; and the Congress may by law provide for the case wherein neither a President elect nor a Vice President shall have qualified, declaring who shall then act as President, or the manner in which one who is to act shall be selected, and such person shall act accordingly until a President or Vice President shall have qualified.

SECTION 4.

The Congress may by law provide for the case of the death of any of the persons from whom the House of Representatives may choose a President whenever the right of choice shall have devolved upon them, and for the case of the death of any of the persons from whom the Senate may choose a Vice President whenever the right of choice shall have devolved upon them.

SECTION 5.

Sections 1 and 2 shall take effect on the 15th day of October following the ratification of this article.

SECTION 6.

This article shall be inoperative unless it shall have been ratified as an amendment to the Constitution by the legislatures of three-fourths of the several States within seven years from the date of its submission.

Amendment XXI

Passed by Congress February 20, 1933. Ratified December 5, 1933.

SECTION 1.

The eighteenth article of amendment to the Constitution of the United States is hereby repealed.

SECTION 2.

The transportation or importation into any State, Territory, or Possession of the United States for delivery or use therein of intoxicating liquors, in violation of the laws thereof, is hereby prohibited.

SECTION 3.

This article shall be inoperative unless it shall have been ratified as an amendment to the Constitution by conventions in the several States, as provided in the Constitution, within seven years from the date of the submission hereof to the States by the Congress.

Amendment XXII

Passed by Congress March 21, 1947. Ratified February 27, 1951.

SECTION 1.

No person shall be elected to the office of the President more than twice, and no person who has held the office of President, or acted as President, for more than two years of a term to which some other person was elected President shall be elected to the office of President more than once. But this Article shall not apply to any person holding the office of President when this Article was proposed by Congress, and shall not prevent any person who may be holding the office of President, or acting as President, during the term within which this Article becomes operative from holding the office of President or acting as President during the remainder of such term.

SECTION 2.

This article shall be inoperative unless it shall have been ratified as an amendment to the Constitution by the legislatures of three-fourths of the several States within seven years from the date of its submission to the States by the Congress.

Amendment XXIII

Passed by Congress June 16, 1960. Ratified March 29, 1961.

SECTION 1.

The District constituting the seat of Government of the United States shall appoint in such manner as Congress may direct: A number of electors of President and Vice President equal to the whole number of Senators and Representatives in Congress to which the District would be entitled if it were a State, but in no event more than the least populous State; they shall be in addition to those appointed by the States, but they shall be considered, for the purposes of the election of President and Vice President, to be electors appointed by a State; and they shall meet in the District and perform such duties as provided by the twelfth article of amendment.

SECTION 2.

The Congress shall have power to enforce this article by appropriate legislation.

Amendment XXIV

Passed by Congress August 27, 1962. Ratified January 23, 1964.

SECTION 1.

The right of citizens of the United States to vote in any primary or other election for President or Vice President, for electors for President or Vice President, or for Senator or Representative in Congress, shall not be denied or abridged by the United States or any State by reason of failure to pay poll tax or other tax.

SECTION 2.

The Congress shall have power to enforce this article by appropriate legislation.

Amendment XXV

Passed by Congress July 6, 1965. Ratified February 10, 1967.
Note: Article II, section 1, of the Constitution was affected by the 25th amendment.

SECTION 1.

In case of the removal of the President from office or of his death or resignation, the Vice President shall become President.

SECTION 2.

Whenever there is a vacancy in the office of the Vice President, the President shall nominate a Vice President who shall take office upon confirmation by a majority vote of both Houses of Congress.

SECTION 3.

Whenever the President transmits to the President pro tempore of the Senate and the Speaker of the House of Representatives his written declaration that he is unable to discharge the powers and duties of his office, and until he transmits to them a written declaration to the contrary, such powers and duties shall be discharged by the Vice President as Acting President.

SECTION 4.

Whenever the Vice President and a majority of either the principal officers of the executive departments or of such other body as Congress may by law provide, transmit to the President pro tempore of the Senate and the Speaker of the House of Representatives their written declaration that the President is unable to discharge the powers and duties of his office, the Vice President shall immediately assume the powers and duties of the office as Acting President. Thereafter, when the President transmits to the President pro tempore of the Senate and the Speaker of the House of Representatives his written declaration that no inability exists, he shall resume the powers and duties of his office unless the Vice President and a majority of either the principal officers of the executive department or of such other body as Congress may by law provide, transmit within four days to the President pro tempore of the Senate and the Speaker of the House of Representatives their written declaration that the President is unable to discharge the powers and duties of his office. Thereupon Congress shall decide the issue, assembling within forty-eight hours for that purpose if not in session. If the Congress, within twenty-one days after receipt of the latter written declaration, or, if Congress is not in session, within twenty-one days after Congress is required to assemble, determines by two-thirds vote of both Houses that the President is unable to discharge the powers and duties of his office, the Vice President shall continue to discharge the same as Acting President; otherwise, the President shall resume the powers and duties of his office.

Amendment XXVI

Passed by Congress March 23, 1971. Ratified July 1, 1971.
Note: Amendment 14, section 2, of the Constitution was modified by section 1 of the 26th amendment.

SECTION 1.

The right of citizens of the United States, who are eighteen years of age or older, to vote shall not be denied or abridged by the United States or by any State on account of age.

SECTION 2.

The Congress shall have power to enforce this article by appropriate legislation.

Amendment XXVII

Originally proposed Sept. 25, 1789. Ratified May 7, 1992.

No law, varying the compensation for the services of the Senators and Representatives, shall take effect, until an election of representatives shall have intervened.

Author's Summary of the Bill of Rights

TWENTY-SEVEN AMENDMENTS HAVE BEEN ADDED to the Constitution since 1789.

Our Founding Fathers realized that the rights contained in the Constitution should be enumerated, spelled out, and thoughtfully defined.

The first ten amendments, known as the Bill of Rights, were adopted as a unit in 1791.

Although the federal government is required by the provisions of the Constitution to respect the individual citizen's basic rights, such as the right of trial by jury (Article I, Sec. 9), the most significant guarantees for individual civil rights were provided by ratification of the Bill of Rights (Amendments 1-10).

The First Amendment guarantees freedom of religion, speech, and the press, the rights of peaceful assembly and petition of the Government.

There are other amendments that protect private property, fair treatment of those accused of crimes, prohibition of unreasonable search and seizure, freedom from self-incrimination, a speedy and impartial jury trial, and representation by counsel.

Without these succinct guidelines, the Constitution would be prone to constant re-definition and interpretation. Consequently, these very first-class laws have become the protections and the important principles that guard us and make us safe as citizens of the United States of America.

The previous pages have contained a number of the democratic principles from which our country was founded, and the basic laws that have kept us a free nation.

CHAPTER FIVE

The Ten Commandments

LAWS TO GOVERN MAN ARE not a recent invention. The first person who created a codex of laws for social behavior was King Ur-Namma in 2100 BCE.

As the legend reports, the god Enlil inspired Ur-Namma to establish laws for the Sumerian city of Urim in order to bring order and prosperity in a hostile and rebellious land.

Then, in 1900 BCE, a lowly shepherd, Lipit-Ishtar, became a prince of Urin and was instructed, once again, through the divine guidance of the gods Anu and Enlil, to create a code of laws to establish justice and fair play in Sumaria and turn back a rebellion.

In 1700 BCE, Hammurabi, the Priest-King of Babylon (formerly Sumaria) inspired by the gods Marduk and Shamish, developed and expanded a codex of laws numbering 282. This codex of Hammurabi is currently the earliest known complete set of laws for the people.

But what about the laws from the god of Abraham? The *Ten Commandments*, also known as the *Decalogue*, are a listing of some of the most important behavioral rules ever stated. They have historically been accepted as the societal rules of conduct, which the god of our Founding Fathers commanded all to follow.

In approximately 1300 BCE, the Torah records that God gave the Decalogue to Moses on Mount Sinai, inscribed on stone tablets, and these Laws were intended for the permanent guidance of the Hebrews.

The founders of the United States of America were mostly deists. They believed in a supreme power who had given them free will, but they did not favor any organized religious system. In spite of that viewpoint, they held in high regard the ancient Mosaic Law for their logic and good sense.

Through the years, exactly what God requires of us remains vague. Most of the laws set forth in Leviticus, Numbers and Deuteronomy are no longer considered literally, no longer practical, no longer applicable or binding in today's world. In the Talmud, the basis of Jewish rabbinic religious authority, there are nearly 25 commandments and over 600 laws!

That said, most Jews and Christians continue to embrace the *Ten Commandments* of the *Decalogue* as central in their lives. Within Islam, the religion's holy book the Qur'an refers to the *Decalogue* and urges that these rules be followed.

There is more than one version of the *Ten Commandments*. And, there are several different traditions regarding how the commands should be enumerated. Jewish tradition considers verse 2 ("I am the Lord your God") to be the first commandment and verses 3-4 ("no gods before Me" and "no idols") as the second. Roman Catholic and Lutheran traditions consider verses 3-4 to be the first commandment but separate verse 17 ("don't covet your neighbor's house; don't covet your neighbor's wife") into two commandments. Protestant and Reformed traditions consider verse 2 a prologue and separate verses 3-4 into the first and second commandments, retaining verse 17 as one command.

The commandments have a specific structure. The first four deal with one's relationship with God. The remaining commandments address one's relationship with humans. The two relationships are inseparable elements, fundamental to being a follower of God.

When asked what the greatest commandment was (Matt. 22:34-40; Mark 12:28-34), Jesus actually quoted the Shema, "You shall love the Lord your God with all your heart, with all your soul and with all your mind" (Deut. 6:5) and Lev. 19:18, "You shall love your neighbor as yourself." Although neither of these are in the Ten Commandments, they summarize their content. "Love God" is equivalent to the first four commandments, and "love your neighbor" is equivalent to the last six.

The following three versions of the Ten Commandments reflect the basic laws for living according to the Jewish and Christian traditions that have so influenced concepts of society and governance in the West.

THE TEN COMMANDMENTS

Hebrew

1. I am the Lord thy God, who brought thee out of the land of Egypt, out of the house of slavery.

2. Thou shalt have no other gods before Me. Thou shalt not make unto thee a graven image, nor any manner of likeness, of any thing that is in heaven above, or that is in the earth beneath, or that is in the water under the earth; Thou shalt not bow down unto them, nor serve them; for I the Lord thy G-d am a jealous God, visiting the iniquity of the fathers upon the children unto the third and fourth generation of them that hate Me; And showing mercy unto the thousandth generation of them that love Me and keep My commandments.

3. Thou shalt not take the name of the Lord thy G-d in vain; for the Lord will not hold him guiltless that taketh His name in vain.

4. Remember the Sabbath day to keep it holy. Six days shalt thou labour, and do all thy work. But the seventh day is the Sabbath in honour of the Lord, thy G-d; on it thou shalt not do any work, neither thou, nor thy son, nor thy daughter, thy manservant nor thy maidservant, nor thy cattle, nor thy stranger that is within thy gates; For in six days the Lord made the heavens and the earth, the sea, and all that is in them, and rested on the seventh day; therefore the Lord blessed the Sabbath day, and hallowed it.

5. Honour thy father and thy mother; in order that thy days may be prolonged upon the land which the Lord thy G-d giveth thee.

6. Thou shalt not kill.

7. Thou shalt not commit adultery.

8. Thou shalt not steal.

9. Thou shalt not bear false witness against thy neighbor.

10. Thou shalt not covet thy neighbor's house; thou shalt not covet thy neighbour's wife, nor his manservant, nor his maidservant, nor his ox, nor his ass, nor any thing that is thy neighbor's.

THE TEN COMMANDMENTS

Catholic

1. I am the Lord thy God. Thou shalt not have strange gods before me.

2. Thou shalt not take the name of the Lord thy God in vain.

3. Remember thou keep the Sabbath Day.

4. Honor thy Father and thy Mother.

5. Thou shalt not kill.

6. Thou shalt not commit adultery.

7. Thou shalt not steal.

8. Thou shalt not bear false witness against thy neighbor.

9. Thou shalt not covet thy neighbor's wife.

10. Thou shalt not covet thy neighbor's goods.

THE TEN COMMANDMENTS

Protestant

1.Thou shalt have no other gods before me.

2. Thou shalt not make unto thee any graven image, or any likeness of any thing that is in heaven above, or that is in the earth beneath, or that is in the water under the earth: Thou shalt not bow down thyself to them, nor serve them: for I the Lord thy God am a jealous God, visiting the iniquity of the fathers upon the children unto the third and fourth generation of them that hate me; And showing mercy unto thousands of them that love me, and keep my commandments.

3. Thou shalt not take the name of the Lord thy God in vain: for the Lord will not hold him guiltless that taketh his name in vain.

4. Remember the sabbath day, to keep it holy. Six days shalt thou labor, and do all thy work: But the seventh day is the sabbath of the Lord thy God: in it thou shalt not do any work, thou, nor thy son, nor thy daughter, thy manservant, nor thy maidservant, nor thy cattle, nor thy stranger that is within thy gates: For in six days the Lord made heaven and earth, the sea, and all that in them is, and rested the seventh day: wherefore the Lord blessed the sabbath day, and hallowed it.

5. Honor thy father and thy mother: that thy days may be long upon the land which the Lord thy God giveth thee.

6. Thou shalt not kill.

7. Thou shalt not commit adultery.

8. Thou shalt not steal.

9. Thou shalt not bear false witness against thy neighbor.

10. Thou shalt not covet thy neighbor's house, thou shalt not covet thy neighbor's wife, nor his manservant, nor his maidservant, nor his ox, nor his ass, nor any thing that is thy neighbor's.

CHAPTER SIX

Patriotic Music

IT HAS BEEN SAID THAT music is the universal language. All people, everywhere, are inspired by music. It is no wonder that patriotic music and great lyrics have always been with us in this country and have become a cherished part of life in America.

American music, in all forms, has very much become the music of the world. Our country is famous for its music. Some great songs were so moving and so widely held in approval that they have become identified with America, and American history.

The inspiration for this kind of music came from the hearts and souls of the songwriters, and from America itself. The composers were so genuinely inspired that they set their feelings to music for Americans to sing and remember their pride and faith in their country.

Of the hundreds of songs written about the United States of America, the following few may be the most memorable. The devotion we have for our great country begins with our Pledge of Allegiance on the following page. Next comes our National Anthem and we move forward through the years revealing "America's Greatest Hit" songs.

Can you sing all of these Golden Oldies?

THE PLEDGE OF ALLEGIANCE

The Pledge of Allegiance, has had the 'editor's pen' thrust at it a few times, but the meaning seems to stand-up well, even with revisions.

Note: [*text in brackets*] indicates the words added on the dates stated above.

ORIGINALLY WRITTEN IN 1892 BY FRANCIS BELLAMY AND/OR JAMES UPHAM

I pledge allegiance to my Flag,
and the Republic for which it stands:
one Nation indivisible,
With Liberty and Justice for all.

REVISED JUNE 14, 1923

I pledge allegiance [to the] Flag of the United States,
and [to] the Republic for which it stands:
one Nation indivisible,
With Liberty and Justice for all.

REVISED JUNE 14, 1924

I pledge allegiance to the Flag
of the United States [of America],
and to the Republic for which it stands:
one Nation indivisible,
With Liberty and Justice for all.

REVISED JUNE 14, 1954

I pledge allegiance to the Flag
of the United States of America
and to the Republic for which it stands,
one nation [under God], indivisible,
with liberty and justice for all.

The National Anthem

WRITTEN BY FRANCIS SCOTT KEY ON SEPTEMBER 14TH, 1814.

Oh, say, can you see, by the dawn's early light,
What so proudly we hailed at the twilight's last gleaming?
Whose broad stripes and bright stars, thro' the perilous fight'
O'er the ramparts we watched, were so gallantly streaming.

And the rockets red glare, the bombs bursting in air,
Gave proof through the night that our flag was still there.
Oh, say, does that star-spangled banner yet wave
O'er the land of the free and the home of the brave?

On the shore dimly seen, thro' the mists of the deep,
Where the foe's haughty host in dread silence reposes,
What is that which the breeze, o'er the towering steep,
As it fitfully blows, half conceals, half discloses?

Now it catches the gleam of the morning's first beam,
In full glory reflected, now shines on the stream;
'Tis the star-spangled banner: oh, long may it wave
O'er the land of the free and the home of the brave.

And where is that band who so vauntingly swore
That the havoc of war and the battle's confusion
A home and a country should leave us no more?
Their blood has wash'd out their foul footstep's pollution.

No refuge could save the hireling and slave
From the terror of flight or the gloom of the grave,
And the star-spangled banner in triumph doth wave
O'er the land of the free and the home of the brave.

Oh, thus be it ever when free men shall stand,
Between their loved homes and the war's desolation;
Blest with vict'ry and peace, may the heav'n-rescued land
Praise the Power that has made and preserved us as a na-
tion.

Then conquer we must, when our cause is just,
And this be our motto: "In God is our trust";
And the star-spangled banner in triumph shall wave
O'er the land of the free and the home of the brave.

Yankee Doodle

EARLIEST KNOWN VERSION 1755—AUTHOR(S) UNKNOWN

Yankee Doodle went to town
A-riding on a pony,
Stuck a feather in his cap
And called it macaroni'.

Yankee Doodle keep it up,
Yankee Doodle dandy,
Mind the music and the step,
And with the girls be handy.

Fath'r and I went down to camp,
Along with Captain Gooding,
And there we saw the men and boys
As thick as hasty puddin'.

Yankee Doodle keep it up,
Yankee Doodle dandy,
Mind the music and the step,
And with the girls be handy.

And there we saw a thousand men
As rich as Squire David,
And what they wasted every day,
I wish it could be saved.

Yankee Doodle keep it up,
Yankee Doodle dandy,
Mind the music and the step,
And with the girls be handy.

And there I see a swamping gun
Large as a log of maple,
Upon a deuced little cart,
A load for father's cattle.

Yankee Doodle keep it up,
Yankee Doodle dandy,
Mind the music and the step,
And with the girls be handy.

And every time they shoot it off,
It takes a horn of powder,
and makes a noise like father's gun,
Only a nation louder.

...and about 10 more verses!

You're A Grand Old Flag

WRITTEN BY GEORGE M. COHAN IN 1906

You're a grand old flag,
You're a high flying flag
And forever in peace may you wave.
You're the emblem of
The land I love.
The home of the free and the brave.

Ev'ry heart beats true
'neath the Red, White and Blue,
Where there's never a boast or brag.
Should auld acquaintance be forgot,
Keep your eye on the grand old flag.

America the Beautiful

WRITTEN BY KATHERINE LEE BATES IN 1913

O' beautiful for spacious skies,
For amber waves of grain,
For purple mountain majesties
Above the fruited plain!

America! America!
God shed his grace on thee
And crown thy good with brotherhood
From sea to shining sea!

O' beautiful for pilgrim feet
Whose stern, impassioned stress
A thoroughfare for freedom beat
Across the wilderness!

America! America!
God mend thine every flaw,
Confirm thy soul in self-control,
Thy liberty in law!

O' beautiful for heroes proved in liberating strife.
Who more than self the country loved
And mercy more than life!

America! America!
May God thy gold refine
Till all success be nobleness
And every gain divine!

O' beautiful for patriot dream
That sees beyond the years
Thine alabaster cities gleam
Undimmed by human tears!

America! America!
God shed his grace on thee
And crown thy good with brotherhood
From sea to shining sea!

God Bless America

WRITTEN BY IRVING BERLIN IN 1918

While the storm clouds gather far across the sea,
Let us swear allegiance to a land
that's free.

Let us all be grateful for a land so fair,
As we raise our voices in a
solemn prayer:

God bless America, land that I love,
Stand beside her and guide her
Through the night with a light from above.

From the mountains, to the prairies,
To the oceans white with foam,

God bless America,
My home sweet home.

This Land Is My Land

WRITTEN BY WOODROW WILSON (WOODY) GUTHRIE IN
1945

This land is your land, this land is my land
From the Redwood Forest to the New York Island
The Canadian mountain to the Gulf Stream waters
This land is made for you and me.

As I go walking this ribbon of highway
I see above me this endless skyway
And all around me the wind keeps saying:
This land is made for you and me.

I roam and I ramble and I follow my footsteps
Till I come to the sands of her mineral desert
The mist is lifting and the voice is saying:
This land is made for you and me.

Where the wind is blowing I go a strolling
The wheat field waving and the dust a rolling
The fog is lifting and the wind is saying:
This land is made for you and me.

Nobody living can ever stop me
As I go walking my freedom highway
Nobody living can make me turn back
This land is made for you and me.

God Bless the U.S.A.

WRITTEN BY LEE GREENWOOD IN 1983

If tomorrow all the things were gone
I'd worked for all my life,
And I had to start again with just my children and my wife.
I'd thank my lucky stars to be living here today,
'Cause the flag still stands for freedom
and they can't take that away.

And I'm proud to be an American where
at least I know I'm free.
And I won't forget the men who died,
who gave that right to me.
And I'd gladly stand up next to you
and defend her still today.
'Cause there ain't no doubt I love this land
God bless the U.S.A.

From the lakes of Minnesota, to the hills of Tennessee,
across the plains of Texas,
From sea to shining sea,

From Detroit down to Houston and New York to LA, Well,
there's pride in every American heart,
and it's time to stand and say:

I'm proud to be an American
where at least I know I'm free.
And I won't forget the men who died,
who gave that right to me.
And I'd gladly stand up next to you
and defend her still today.
'Cause there ain't no doubt I love this land
God bless the U.S.A.

CHAPTER SEVEN

A Voice of Reason

CURRENTLY, HONESTY AND INTEGRITY ARE not easily found in the American media. Sadly, the reporting of news has become very questionable, and far from factual.

At present, we are receiving a dangerous kind of biased history, mixed with the daily news from a very commercial media that often cares little about the truth.

Does our government really control what we see and hear? Well, it wouldn't be the first time that the citizens of a country were fed only what a government wanted them to hear and they heard that propaganda and believed it all.

In the not so recent past the governments of Russia, Germany, China, Japan, North Korea, Italy, Argentina, Cuba and most of the Middle Eastern countries have manipulated the media and re-written history to their liking. Sadly, their citizens never got to hear the truth. Causing that to happen is not as difficult as it seems. One infamous leader stated that: "It's a good thing for governments that the people are so stupid."

The infamous Adolph Hitler made that quote. With a small, yet very effective, government, he nearly conquered the world. Could that happen to us?

Well, if you combine well-planned print propaganda with powerful oration on radio and television, and fill it in with phony conviction, enthusiasm, and repetition, you have a sure-fire propaganda formula that will successfully give you control over the People.

Can it happen again?

Today, in the United States of America, manipulated propaganda has replaced an honest media. Every day, we are confused and barraged with erroneous bits of information. It is difficult to determine what is true.

We must not fall prey to those who wish to have absolute power over America and the world. In order for them to accomplish their plan, they must first wrest our freedom and liberty away from us. We must not allow that.

Freedom should be ongoing and guaranteed, but the payment for our liberty is constant attentiveness and individual participation. Acta non verba!

We are still permitted to disagree and to dissent. Despite our freedom, an appropriate description of the current general attitude of the American People is blithe, blasé and befuddled.

You may wonder who I am and why I'm talking this way. Well, I'm just an interested 'nobody;' an American citizen who has never been involved with politics or any political party in my entire life. Never, that is, until I started a radio program called: The Voice of Reason.

I had questions and was tired of the talk-talk--shout-shout biased radio shows and wanted to hear from the People on issues that mattered to them.

Unfortunately, I heard very little honesty from the People and had to listen to lot of opinion, prejudice and dogma from amateur political supporters.

As the host of The Voice of Reason radio program I wanted to find out why the average American citizen always talked about the issues, e.g., inflation, high gas prices, poverty, wars, invasion of privacy, government corruption, etc., but didn't do anything about those problems!

They talked and grumbled, they criticized and found fault with everything, yet did nothing to correct the problems.

The American public is always whining and they'll complain about anything, to anyone, anytime. But mostly, they never do anything about their troubles.

Is this widespread un-involvement and apathy the cause of us losing our liberties and becoming a neurotic nation?

Here's a fact: Each time we elect the same kind of politicians we get the same outcome. That's not neurosis... that's insanity*.

*The definition of insanity is doing the same thing over and over and expecting different results. --Benjamin Franklin

American's think they are in charge but in fact, they will always do what they are told to do. Today, they're still being conned and are rapidly losing their money, their freedoms, their liberty, their privacy, and their self-respect.

We're stuck in a rut and have forgotten it's our right to speak-out and that we also have the great privilege and responsibility to correct our own problems.

Surely, the American people are not still waiting for the government to fix their troubles. Or are we?

It could be that these great "get up-get going" Americans have stopped getting-up, and are going nowhere. Or, maybe they're confused, or frightened, or asleep?

I have followed the passing political parade since I first began to comprehend it. But, I've always wondered why our great democratic system doesn't exactly perform like Madison, Adams and Jefferson envisioned it ought to work.

Early in my life, I suffered a nasty political trauma. Post World War II, in the 1950's, I was a teenager. I listened to the old-style patriotic statements and learned and held to the traditional beliefs of history that was being taught during that decade.

One day I read a magazine article about how Harry Truman got elected as a U.S. Senator from Kansas.

Sadly, I learned that Kansas City political boss Thomas Pendergast and his mob boys had stuffed the ballot boxes to elect ol' Harry.

Well, that did it for me. Total disillusionment.

I had been taught and believed, that our voting system was above reproach and an incident like the Truman/Pendergast deal was not only astounding and I thought it not American-like at all.

My faith was shattered. I was young and very naïve.

I read that travesty of fairness and began to wonder about our alleged democratic voting system and whether it was, or ever had been, fair and honest.

Though some of the Pendergast mob were later sent to Federal prisons [on other charges], I felt even more contempt for the system when Harry Truman gave each of them a Presidential pardon as he left office. Sounded corrupt and unethical at that time, and it still does!

Somewhere in the 50's I saw two Frank Capra films: "Mr. Smith Goes To Washington" and "Meet John Doe". Wow, I thought: The great American Spirit was still alive!

After seeing Capra's films I was rejuvenated and inspired. Even though corruption was out there waiting for us, I thought, American justice would prevail. Boy, I was not only naïve, but very uninformed.

I got to see how they sold the WWII hero Dwight D. Eisenhower on TV to a very gullible public. Ike had no political background, but you Liked Ike. He was the first political TV celebrity. The first mass selling of a president!

I began to read a little history and understood that politics was a dirty, lying, corrupt and unfair game and that politicians most times took care of their cronies and the big power mongers. They did very little to address the needs or wants of the people, and today, it's still that way.

In the 60's, I read quite a lot and wanted to learn more about this election that the government puts on every four years. I hoped some-day to find out if anyone could reverse the imbalance of power: Them versus Us.

During the next decade, another war hero, John Kennedy, also with little political background, got the ballot boxes stuffed by the Chicago mob and became president.

And, let's not forget the stories of the "King Fish" Huey Long, or LBJ's Texas corruption or our anger about Korea, Viet Nam, the JFK, MLK, RFK assassinations, Nixon's Watergate, Reagan's Iran-Contra scandal and today, 911, the War on Terrorism and Bush's immoral inva-sion and occupation of Iraq and Afghanistan.

These events have not been the brightest periods in American his-tory and there have been many more incidents wrought with greed and noticeable dishonesty.

America does have a checkered past.

It sure appears as though the people's voice [the vote] just might be an old-fashioned "ruse" to keep us happy and unaware of the real deal.

And today, more than ever, the deal, it keeps-a-changin'.

But, in spite of all that, I still have faith. Faith in the concept I guess, and that the great idea that our "American Dream" is alive and beats on in the hearts of the People.

To you who believe in this dream, if you understand, that freedom will continue for all of us. Please remember that:

There are those that make things happen.

There are those who watch things happen.

There are those who say: What happened?

I give you this warning: Doing nothing can be extremely hazardous to your future. Get involved now and make our elected representatives do the work they were appointed and promised they would to do.

Over these many years I've never stopped talking about "the way it is" and "the way it oughta be", to my friends, my family and to just about anyone who would listen to me. To be sure, I can be quite a bore on that subject.

Back in 1971, I was visiting a lawyer friend at his retirement home. He was in his late eighties and had been a long time political campaigner, associated with his party for well over sixty years. I enjoyed speaking with him for he was very informed and extremely intelligent. Whenever I had the opportunity to talk with this insightful man, I learned.

On that particular day of my visit we were talking politics and law, as usual, and I said: Isn't it a shame that a sincere, honest man of the people can't get elected to the presidency? It seemed to me that such a man could clean house and return our government to the control of fair and honest representatives of the American people.

I naively asked him: What could be done to make this happen? It was sort of a loaded question, but I eagerly waited to hear his answer.

The old man laughed and said that it was a nice idea. Impossible -but nice. He flatly said it couldn't happen, because my ideal candidate's political party absolutely would not allow it to happen.

I pushed on and said what if this "good man" lied to the party, did exactly as they directed, got elected and appeared to play ball with them, but in fact, he had a hidden agenda, and plans of his own design to make a difference.

This wise old man interrupted me and said your 'miracle man' could never reach the top without being discovered by the party, or someone, and if he were found out, they'd pull the rug from under him. They'd ruin him.

I persisted and told him that "my man" would be very clever and very cooperative to the party bosses, and then when he became president, he'd make moves to create changes in government policies so that, ultimately, the American people would benefit more than ever before.

He smiled and quietly told me that a couple of young brothers tried to do that a few years ago, and they shot both of them, -dead!

Well, that answered that!

Journalist H.L. Mencken hit the nail on the head: "All government, of course, is against liberty".

So, today we still need to clean house. Get rid of those who are corrupt. Simply put: Don't "re-hire" those who will not represent you and don't vote for anyone who has special interests and a bad track record. But how?

First, don't let them confuse you, and don't give up.

As citizens, we must keep an eye on these "grand and glorious" representatives of the people, and constantly remind them that: They work for us!

Our elected representatives need to hear from their constituents, ... and we shouldn't mince words!

If you want a better future you must get involved. Let them hear from "We, the People" and, by the way, don't just talk about it, do something about it!

Let these politicians know that we want changes. Make a real effort. You've got to stay on their backs. Be relentless!

Contact them in person, call them on the phone, mail and email and fax them. Do all of these things, and then do them again, and again!

As Americans, we need to speak-out. But this time we must not merely complain and point fingers, or site the obvious or make fun of them.

We have to think before we speak and mean what we say!

We need to come up with ideas of how to fix these problems. Think of it: Just one good idea might inspire a man or women to make things better for all of us.

Today, we are living with a very serious predicament. We are currently involved in the most dangerous and incredible "power politics" that has ever been seen in our country.

Both Parties want permanent control of the government for their own causes and interests and will do anything, ethical, or not, to accomplish this.

Political competition for control has gone on for a long time. It is a very old game with nothing new.

Currently, we have an unprecedented possibility that one side will gain such a powerful position that the losing party will become impotent, becoming a party in name only.

When a president has strong control over the Congress and the Supreme Court we have lost the separation of the three branches of government and freedom ceases to exist.

If we allow that to happen, that would mean a one-party system has taken power, and that my friends will spell the end of freedom, liberty and justice as promised to us in our Constitution and Bill of Rights.

Some of the most infamous men of the last century Mussolini, Hitler, Franco, Stalin, Idi Amin, Pinochet, Pol Pot, Mao, Saddam Hussein,

Mubarak, Gaddafi gained power over their own people and became dictators.

The people of those countries allowed autocratic governments to emerge, with one decision maker leading one-party with the intention of controlling the people.

These dictators were extremely cruel and powerful rulers.

And, whether we know it or not, if we don't stay awake, we could end up with a dictator of our own!

CHAPTER EIGHT

Some American History

OUR FOUNDING FATHERS UNDERSTOOD THAT disharmony and conflict with our government quickly becomes the friction that slows the wheels of tyranny and oppression.

For us to dissent is the only way to save our democracy.

The American people need to again take charge of their country and remember that *We*, not the politicians, have the final word concerning our future.

The people of the world have observed our apathetic acceptance of the widespread corruption in our own government. They are confused, for the government of the United States says one thing, and does another.

Acta non verba, is what our Founding Fathers would have done. These men did not like tyranny or oppression, and didn't just talk or write about it, they fought against it!

When he was hailed as the "Father of the Constitution," Madison emphatically protested that *the document was not the off-spring of a single brain, but the work of many heads and many hands.*

These were very intelligent and far-thinking men and they saw the opportunity during their lifetimes to create what has been called "The Great Experiment In Liberty."

Thomas Jefferson observed: *When the people fear their government, there is tyranny; when the government fears the people, there is liberty.*

James Madison, Thomas Jefferson and John Adams appear to be the foundation of what American freedom means. Their words and ideologies are timeless.

Although reading the works of these great men will take some time, it is worth it, for their unique ideas are as powerful now as when they were first conceived.

With a great amount of input from Madison, Hamilton, Adams and others, Thomas Jefferson penned the *Declaration of Independence* and later on, as the *Constitution* was being framed, he made strong suggestions that this new Constitution should, in fact, have a *Bill of Rights* in order to clarify and safeguard future freedoms of the people.

The Bill of Rights and its amendments, stands today as the founders envisioned it, as a special protection of the rights of the American Citizen.

If Washington was the *Sword and Father of our Country*, Madison, Adams and Jefferson were the *mind and soul and conscience*. They were realists, not idealists.

Although Jefferson was reluctant to become president, he was elected for two terms. During his tenure, Jefferson expanded our new country with the very wise purchase of the Louisiana territory from France.

And, Jefferson directed Lewis and Clark to chart and define the boundaries of this vast country from coast to coast. In addition he laid the groundwork and principles for all presidents that succeeded him.

After his presidency, Jefferson retired to Virginia at Monticello, his home and estate, and began to finish an earlier dream, the design and construction of the University of Virginia. Jefferson never stopped thinking or working.

In these latter years he wrote his autobiography and corresponded with John Adams with some of the most amazing and meaningful words ever written about America. These writings between the two men are considered to be some of their most far-reaching and brilliant comments.

Albeit a difficult birth in 1776, with all of its promises of justice, freedom and liberty, the United States of America was born to inspire all men, everywhere.

Because of that beginning, no other civilization in history has enjoyed the freedoms we have today.

Most free societies have not existed for long, as the light of freedom diminishes very quickly.

Previous to the formation of the United State of America, very powerful and oppressive monarchs ruled harshly over the people and the nations of the world.

In those days, the people expected their masters to provide them with protection from invading enemies. For this security, they were compelled to abide by the mostly unjust sets of laws as dictated by their rulers. These unfortunate people had no say regarding the conditions of how they would work or live.

Taxing the people was one of the ways the old rulers maintained control. The people worked hard and paid unreasonable taxes to the king. They were left with little to live on and if they refused to pay their taxes, their property was confiscated and they were imprisoned in order to make an example to the rest of the population.

Sounds like our own dear, sweet IRS, doesn't it?

The Founding Fathers of America had a great revulsion of this unfair kind of government, and that is most likely why they developed the concepts of "Liberty and Justice For All."

Our founders didn't like King George III's laws and his unjust treatment of his subjects, and therefore decided to create a nation where the people could in an organized and equitable manner rule themselves and forever be free of tyranny and oppressive cruelty and to live in peace without government or religious persecution.

In his latter years, Jefferson reflected on what they had accomplished. Even though the *Constitution* and its *Bill of Rights* were filled with the best ideas they could conceive, he still had some misgivings and gave further advice and warnings to future generations.

He said: *The effort, now, will be to keep the wolves from the sheep*, and warned us *not to allow the government become too powerful over the people.*

Jefferson also said: *The tree of liberty must be refreshed from time to time with the blood of patriots, and tyrants.*

Yes, Jefferson was poignant, yet logical. It seems that this man was not only creative, intelligent and idiosyncratic for his time, but he may have also been an early futurist; maybe even a prophet!

Today, these words, if not coming from one of the Founding Fathers, would sound treasonous, wouldn't they? But Jefferson and the others were men of reason and logic, as well as fearless and optimistic leaders.

They understood human nature and that man has always had a desire to control man –to play God. They knew that in the future their brilliant concept of a representative government might give way to tyranny and oppression.

So each of them gave us warnings, the chief being that our government would some day turn on us; becoming harsh and tyrannical. I believe that day is nearly upon us.

Now, we have less and less to say about the way our country operates. There are more and more laws, most of which are intended to bind and control us, not to treat us fairly or to protect us.

Taxes seem to be out of control. Could our Founding Fathers even imagine the taxes that the American people are forced to pay, and that if they don't pay their taxes, they're put in jail, losing their liberty and forfeiting their property to the government.

Debtors prisons again?

And those that we consider the Representatives of the People mostly ignore us and take care of their special interests in order to line their pockets with gold.

The caste system has returned. The wealthy govern, and the new class of "technocrats" do their bidding because they are constantly in fear of losing their positions and being reduced to a lower economic level.

Unfortunately, we are all still slaves to the rich. And, as always, the wealth is made on the backs of the people, and the profits are denied to the workers.

There is no "trickle-down economy." The money and the power still remain at the top. Most of us grew up believing that sort of oppressiveness was not to be in the United States, but apparently it is a thing that will not die.

The strong, powerful, government idea continues and our two-party arrangement is in real jeopardy of becoming a one-party system with authoritarian rule.

We have only a little time to correct the grievous errors that our politicians are committing against us. We must wake them up now, or we may never have the chance again.

Currently, Americans are taught to believe we have:

More privately-owned cars and housing.

The most national and personal wealth.

More airlines, trains and buses.

The largest public educational system.

The greatest military might.

The best medical system.

Great abundance of natural resources.

The biggest industries and food producers.

A profusion of innovative thinkers.

We believe that we have it all, and the rest of the world is without and should be quite envious. We think that most nations would like to have a system such as ours, one that is free, creative, industrious and prosperous. But is it?

We no longer have the most cars, our public transportation system is in shambles, our military is mighty but vulnerable, our educational system ranks poorly against other nations, our health care system is the laughing stock of the world, we no longer have the biggest industries, our national and personal wealth is in bankruptcy, our innovation lacks commitment and our inventive thinkers are rapidly coming from other countries as we dumb down our own people.

Our natural resources are rapidly depleting, and we have become the biggest polluters of the environment in history. The USA is not the vanguard of the world.

Our country does not have an equitable arrangement for dispensing its wealth to its own people.

All that glitters is not gold; the truth can be depressing.

The perception that the United States of America is the richest nation could, by another measure, be considered the poorest country in the world.

The citizens of the United States of America should be getting a better share of this great national abundance than they are receiving. They are being cheated by big businesses and our own government.

The opportunity to correct this may be about to go away.

If history repeats itself, *We, The People* are currently losing and the rich, again, are winning!

CHAPTER NINE

Many Questions

HOPEFULLY THE FOLLOWING QUESTIONS MIGHT cause you to stop and think about the way things are today.

• Why is our government meddling in the world?
• Why don't we develop affordable alternative energy?
• Why are movies, TV, music & video games confusing our lives?
• Why have we lost our elected representatives to greed?
• Why are we becoming a Police State?
• Why do terrorists want to attack our country?
• Why is there so much poverty and starvation in America?
• Why are our young people afraid to believe in the future?
• Why are the rich getting richer and the poor getting poorer?
• Why is our water and food becoming more and more polluted?
• Why are the big corporations sending our jobs abroad?
• Why aren't our children learning to read and write?
• Why are Americans so neurotic and their children more violent?
• Why isn't health care "free" to anyone who needs it?
• Why do we allow the government to invade our privacy?
• Why are nearly 3 million people in jails in the "land of the free?"
• Why is our government gathering more information on us?
• Why do most of the nations of the world dislike America?
• Why don't we eliminate our very flawed income tax system?
• Why has gambling become the new American pastime?
• Why isn't higher education "free" to all who want it?
• Why are the arts and music programs being eliminated?
• Why don't Americans demand government accountability?
• Will automation replace white and blue-collar workers?
• Will those that are unemployed remain unemployed?
• Will a National ID card save us from the terrorists?
• Is there legal justice, even if you don't have money?

More questions could be added to this list, but even if they are, will *you* actually do anything about correcting these problems? Do you really understand these issues?

Each of the Founding Fathers agreed that in order to have fair and trustworthy representation, we must interact with those we elect. We must keep them honest and aware. Therefore, as citizens, our job is never done.

Why should every American citizen be afforded *Equal* and unvarying *Freedom*? Are we a *Republic* or a *Democracy*? What is *Liberty*? What do these words mean and where did this unique American ideology get its beginnings?

Many of the common words need to be understood in order to know what our founding fathers intended for us.

Here are the definitions of these important words:

Equal: Of the same measure, quantity, amount, as another.

Freedom: The quality or state of being free, the absence of necessity, coercion, or constraint in choice or action, liberation from slavery or restraint or from the power of authority.

Republic: A government having a chief of state who is not a monarch and who in modern times is usually a president. A political unit having such a form of government in which supreme power resides in a body of citizens entitled to vote.

Democracy: A government by the people; especially, rule of the majority, in which the supreme power is vested in the people and exercised by them directly or indirectly through a system of representation, usually involving periodically held free elections.

Liberty: The quality or state of being free, the power to do as one pleases, freedom from physical restraint, freedom from arbitrary or despotic control, the positive enjoyment of various social, political or economic rights and privileges, the power of choice.

These words are the fundamental backbone of our form of government. They embody an affirmation of the rights afforded to all citizens of the United States of America.

The original documents for the preservation and protection of the citizens of United States have become the greatest and most well known writings on the subject of freedom, liberty and justice in the history of mankind.

Ever since the assurances made in these original documents were first written, many nations of the world have read their contents, admired the ideals and have been desirous of adopting these principles for their own citizens.   Some countries have even succeeded in employing this type of democracy and surely, more will do so in the future.

The United States Of America is the greatest nation in the history of the world and it is: The Land of the Free and the Brave--The Enemy of Tyranny--A Country With Compassion and Charity--The Land Of Opportunity--The Land Of Liberty, and surely, it should remain: A Government of the People, by the People and for the People."

All of these great maxims have inspired the sentiments as voiced by Americans throughout our history.

But sometimes we forget who we are and what great gifts of freedom and equality have been given to us by merely being born, or becoming American citizens.

With these inalienable rights comes great responsibility. In order to protect our freedoms we must be ever vigilant.

We must watch those whom we have elected to represent us so they do not achieve supremacy over us, thereby becoming our masters, and we their slaves.

Governments, if not watched and disagreed with, can quickly become totalitarian. The people are then oppressed.

The journalist Dorothy Thompson warned us:

When liberty is taken away by force, it can be restored by force. When it is relinquished voluntarily, by default, it can never be recovered.

There is no doubt that our liberty is quietly being compromised and stolen from us.

Little by little, our freedoms are disappearing. Can we stop it? Is the theft of our liberties intentional?

Well, my Irish grandmother used to say: "Whether you step on me' foot by accident, or on purpose, me' foot still hurts!" Ol' Granny was correct.

So, in fact, we don't really need to know why we are losing our liberties, but we must be aware that they are being lost, and we must stop this loss...now!

The democratic ideas in the Declaration Of Independence, and the details of how this new country might operate, as laid out in the Constitution and its Bill Of Rights, the intention was always to have a government that listened to, and abided by, the will of the people.

The Founders believed that an obedient group of representatives would be a powerful deterrent to prevent the government from becoming oppressive.

In the early formation of this country, the zealous selfishness and aggressiveness of some of his contemporaries bothered Jefferson. Even though he felt that the founding concepts were sound, he worried about human nature. The imminent danger, he felt, was that the government could, someday, become too authoritarian.

He wondered how could it be assured that future leaders would not grow ambitious, greedy and ultimately too powerful? The likelihood of this happening troubled him greatly. The Constitution, although a fine idea, had flaws.

Even the far-seeing Jefferson could not have conceived that in this relatively short period of history, just over two-hundred-forty years, the people's influence would not again be heard and that this magnificently planned democratic government would become an authoritative system and more and more oppressive toward its citizens. These great original ideas of freedom have begun to fail us.

Today, our leaders have become very arrogant and indifferent to the people. Apparently they think they are above reproach and can do as they please.

That's a frightening revelation, but it has happened!

In fact, our government has become quite powerful and oppressive toward its citizens. We, as American people, have either become apathetic, or we're all very stupid. We need to demand our rights before it is too late.

Presently, our city, state and federal leaders, as well as our Congressmen and Senators, the alleged representatives of the people, do not listen to the citizens and basically do as they please as they serve "special interests".

Because of the vast amounts of money involved these elected representatives appear to no longer care about We, the American People. They have become indifferent to our needs. They only serve and cater to the demands of the organized political parties and the private interests of big corporate businesses. They feather their own nests, first.

We have become afraid of our government. Ironically they should fear the citizenry, for there are more than three hundred million of us out here.

Unfortunately, these politicians are in charge of every aspect of our lives. On top of that, we actually pay these men and women unbelievable salaries and perks to support this very powerful government that burdens us with more and more taxes and self-serving laws.

Incredible as it seems, we pay them vast amounts of money to oppress us! This makes absolutely no sense.

In addition to their high salaries, we find that most of them are using their offices to gain millions of dollars more in perks from special interests and corporations.

Our representatives are quite simply crooks and must immediately (if not sooner) be fired from their jobs!

Someone once said that to cite a problem without having a suggestion for an answer is a waste of time.

Well, we have discovered the problem, now we must find the solution.

Can we stop our government's insatiable quest for power over the people?

A Few Answers

MANY ANSWERS ARE NEEDED AND they must come from us. But, we need action, not words.

The prevailing, and sadly incorrect, thinking of most Americans is: "What's the problem? We *are* heard from quite often. We have the vote!"

Yes, we vote. The People speak en masse and then that "very special person" is elected by a consensus of the American people. Yes, we get to vote. The People are allowed to speak and our government is supposed to hear and obey.

Well, there are several things wrong with that good idea.

First of all, the Vote doesn't happen without prejudice or tremendous influence.

The people vote only after being barraged by advertising filled with clever, psychological sound bites, designed to cause you to vote for their attractive and glib candidate, and when you do vote, you have no concept of why you voted, or if your selection was correct.

Was it your own decision, or was it *theirs*.

Clearly, the content and facts are delivered to us for many months [years] prior to the election, via primaries, debates and speeches during the furious campaigning to allow you to remember the faces and some of the facts, as they are spun, so you can make your decision before you vote.

Of course, the comments made during the political campaigns from all sides are intentionally skewed, not fair or balanced or very clear. They want to mix us up!

With radio, television and the Internet being the most powerful message delivery systems in the history of the world, the designers of these political campaigns always enlist the most talented and skilled media manipulators to sell their man or woman to the public.

They buy huge amounts of airtime and put his or her face in our face day after day. The result is that we never know what the candidate, or the incumbent, is really talking about, but we do remember the name and the face. It appears that all of this hoopla is merely show business combined with subliminal marketing.

I'm sure that the politicians believe that the "general vote" will always keep the people happy, and so this ostensible charade goes on every four years, uninterrupted and with extreme confidence for those who pull off it.

In their snobbery, the politicians consider that the average American is too ignorant and incapable of knowing what he really needs for himself.

Of course, they never have asked us, for we might tell them who and what we want, but that could be disastrous.

And, why do all of our politicians use large words, elevated language, double-talk, hyperbole, mudslinging, false statistics and lying? Why can't they talk honestly to the people? Why are they hiding the facts? Why are they afraid to be clear and precise?

The Democrats proclaim that we should have more taxes, more social programs, larger government. They want to give everybody, everything and take care of everybody. This is altruism of the highest order.

In turn, the Republicans counter with wars, lower taxes, less social programs. Favoring big business and smaller government, they tell us "to work for it, if you want it."

In the end, both parties are colossal hypocrites.

Both parties ignore the fact that there is not a level playing field out here. Not all people are prepared or educated to compete in today's society.

However, these very ignored and ineligible people could become productive again and able to fit back into society with a little help and some perceptive, intelligent, and sincere leadership from our government.

The dilemma appears that once these professional politicians are elected by the people, they immediately begin to serve their corporate masters, not the people.

They forget the people's needs, ignore the pressing social issues and continue their double-talk. It doesn't matter, whether Republican or Democrat, as soon as they are elected, they return to business as usual employing their own agendas and promptly ignore us.

They will say anything to get elected and will forget their promises to the people. Then there will be another election and again, nothing substantive done to aid the people.

In the real world, these "good representatives of the people" have reneged on their oaths of office, and therefore should be known as *welshers.*

Alas, we stupid Americans continue to put up with their chicanery thinking it's going to be better this time.

Well, if we don't stop them now, Heaven knows how far they will go, using anything they can, to get absolute power.

Our military/industrial structure, in partnership with our government, *is*, and it should be stated factually, as *Fascist.*

Take a quick look at history and you'll realize that a government that has absolute power, knows no boundaries.

Republican or Democrat, we do have a government who are in league with big business and banking, and are seeking more and more control over the citizens. This authoritarianism is not just a far-fetched idea. It's a reality.

Is it possible that we could get a few politicians to listen to their constituents' needs, and then go to work and actually address those needs?

Is that simple proposition far-fetched?

Sadly, if our representatives did try, those few sincere elected officials would still be controlled by their parties' demands. Quite a conflict of interest, isn't it?

Here are a few more definitions we should remember:

GOVERNMENT: The act or process of governing. The organization, machinery, or agency through which a political unit exercises authority and performs functions.

POLITICS: The art or science concerned with guiding and influencing governmental policy, concerned with winning and holding control over a government.

POLITICIAN: A person experienced in the art or science of government, engaged in party politics as a profession, primarily interested in political office for narrow, unreal, reasons.

The founding fathers thought that our politicians should not be professionals and that they should not be allowed to hold major offices if they were political specialists.

Maybe I'm naïve, but I believe we need are experienced, sensible, honest people to run this country in an effective and business-like manner. What we have are a bunch of selfish, privileged, do-nothing politicians!

Running a city or a state or even the United States is very much like the operation of a business. A business must deal fairly with its management, employees, customers and vendors. Important problems must be solved quickly and accurately, or that business will fail.

The number of problems facing our country are clear and just about anyone could recognize that these are the important issues that they must be solved without delay.

Even though our government recognizes the major problems facing America, unfortunately they are still not being addressed, nor remedied.

The world is looking at us wondering if liberty will live.

Our government seems to have an insatiable appetite for worldwide domination. Maybe it is empire-building?

Our many unsolved domestic issues and our government's penchant for war and imperialism is a humiliation for the people of the United States.

Just in the last six decades, a country that had earned the admiration of every nation in the world is now losing respect. Our reputation is being torn apart. We are no longer looked upon as a strong, kind and benevolent people.

The United States of America is acting like the terrible enemies of democracy that it had fought in the past.

The United States is waging war instead of diplomacy.

The United States is invading and occupying countries.

The United States is corrupting foreign governments

The United States is meddling in affairs of many nations.

The United States is killing innocent people.

The United States is destroying infrastructures.

The United States has become, in the eyes of the world, "The Evil" that all people in history have feared.

It's time to get an entirely new U.S. Congress.

We need an unbiased, non-political U.S. Supreme Court.

The citizens want a fair and responsible U.S. President.

Each time we have an election we must *demand* that our government perform honorable and fair acts. Not war.

Our government must be rational in its decisions and obey the *demands* of its citizens, or *We The People*, will suffer the consequences.

CHAPTER ELEVEN

We Must Act Now

HERE'S A CHECKLIST THAT I put on the back on a few T-shirts a while back. It summarizes some major problems that need to be solved. You might want to make a few of these "walking billboards", yourself.

Dear Politician:
I want the following issues corrected—*NOW!*

[√] MAKE AN END TO MIDDLE EAST WARS
[√] CREATE A GENUINE PLAN FOR ALTERNATIVE ENERGY
[√] FREE HEALTH CARE FOR ALL AMERICANS
[√] STOP SENDING JOBS OUT OF OUR COUNTRY
[√] FIND JOBS FOR ALL AMERICANS WHO WANT TO WORK
[√] ELIMINATE THE WELFARE SYSTEM
[√] INCREASE THE MINIMUM WAGE TO A LIVABLE WAGE
[√] CREATE A SENSIBLE IMMIGRATION PLAN
[√] REPAIR OUR CRUMBLING INFRASTRUCTURE
[√] ELIMINATE POVERTY AND STARVATION IN THE UNITED STATES
[√] STOP THE SURVEILLANCE OF U.S. CITIZENS
[√] CLEAN UP OUR AIR, WATER AND FOOD SYSTEMS
[√] ELIMINATE THE IRS METHOD OF TAXATION
[√] BALANCE NATIONAL AND STATE BUDGETS
[√] GUARANTEE FEDERAL & STATE GOVERNMENT ACCOUNTABILITY
[√] MAKE STRICT TERM LIMITS FOR CONGRESS
[√] OVERHAUL THE WORLD'S IMPRESSION OF THE UNITED STATES

These vital issues are just a few of the many ongoing problems that are, or soon will, involve all Americans.

Unless we act now, these troubles, and more, will be around for a long time. Our goal should be to immediately eliminate these problems for all times.

Stop and think about these issues. After all, it is our country, and therefore, these difficulties belong to all of us!

Each of these problems could be solved with simple implementation. That is, if the necessary actions were not delayed by squabbling from both sides of the aisle. Most of these issues have been in debate, in committee, and under discussion for many, many years. Typically, our representatives do a little work on some of the issues just to impress us that they are still trying. They talk, but most of these problems are never really solved. That's called "sandbagging" or "stonewalling."

Think about it this way. If you were the CEO of a company that had major problems and you did little but talk about those very important issues, you would quickly be fired by your directors for not getting the job done.

Yet, America's major problems go and on, and of course, as in all things left undone, there is a slow and steady accumulation of the "not accomplished" that eventually causes these vital issues to grow larger and larger.

By not solving these major problems in a timely fashion our leaders allow our country to sink deeper and become mired in more and more of the same "do nothingness."

After all, these are merely the basic needs of all people: safety, food, health, housing and employment - simply the things that people need to have a reasonable life. These are not luxuries or unreasonable demands.

All of these issues could be answered by any politician with just a simple: "I promise to immediately correct these serious problems that threaten the comfort, safety and future of the American people."

I assure you that the man or woman who becomes our president in the future and quickly repairs the real problems of the American people will go down in the history books as the greatest leader of modern times.

Both political parties should put away their political leanings and immediately realize that there are no budgets more significant, no issues more important, than helping the American people to maintain safe, reasonable and productive lives. That should be the goal.

These political parties, without partisanship, need to shake hands with each other and go to work to rebuild and rejuvenate our country and not by using pressure, force or bravado but using sincere cooperation between the parties.

These genuine efforts would impress and, once again, gain the true admiration and favor of all Americans and the people of the World, as well.

It's apparent that we Americans need to talk these issues over with each other. We need to agree on solutions to these problems, convey our answers to the government leaders, then, demand that the leaders act to correct the problems.

But how can we all get together without being swayed by the political influences? How can we use our good individual minds to solve these problems?

In the earlier times of our country, the people could get together and discuss, and even argue, about the important issues concerning their city or state.

They held town hall meetings and because they would all be in the same spot at the same time, a majority vote could quickly be achieved on any issue that was being presented.

Even though a true consensus came from those old town hall meetings, Thomas Jefferson realized: "that once outside the town, a democracy turns into a republic."

We need new ideas and new blood and capable and truthful people to correct the mess we are in. We need people who do not "speechify", or propose answers for special interests. We need individuals who do not favor the policies of either political party who will only deal with what the people of the United States need and demand.

Ross Perot was a man who tried to make a difference. During his cross-country campaign, he confirmed that the American People wanted to be fairly represented by a more accountable government. They really wanted 'change'.

In 1992, Ross Perot stated most emphatically:

> *We the people of the United States of America, recognizing that our republic was founded as a government of the people, by the people and for the people, can unite to restore the integrity of the economic and political systems. We must commit ourselves to organize, to educate, to participate in the political process, and to hold our public servants accountable. We shall rebuild our country, renew its economic, moral and social strength, and return the sovereignty of the American People. We The People have*

something more important than lobbyists' money. We
have the vote.

Perot spent millions and millions of his own dollars polling the people. His conclusion was to form a third party that had no allegiance to anyone, or anything, but the people. Sadly, he withdrew from his campaign. Who knows why, but big pressure from the other parties is suspected.

Personally, I don't think we need a third party. The two parties we have are plenty to deal with!

The "third voice" is us, and if we don't make some noise soon, we may end up with a one party system and surely, that party won't want, or allow us to be heard at all.

Oppression. Authoritarianism. Fascism. In America?

Can it happen here? Is it possible? Well, it has happened before, you know. To quote Adolph Hitler: "The people will more easily fall victims to a big lie than to a small one."

Now, that's the vicious voice of a one-party system!

To vote for the party we choose, and to have our votes fairly counted and thereby make our demands heard, that's the great gift of a free society. Fairly counted votes?

The American people need to seriously and continuously address the major issues and loudly give their opinions to our representatives and they need to follow-up to see that their demands are obeyed.

Some of our elected representatives are untrustworthy and selfish people. Their private interests take precedence over the desires and needs of the American people.

Our leaders must stop telling us there are not funds to take care of the American people, and at the same time spend multi-billions yearly on the military, billions monthly on aggressive wars and billions and billions on the occupation and reconstruction of other countries.

Our own country is in very bad condition! Those misspent billions should be used to ensure good living standards, jobs and equality for the American people, as well as the rebuilding of crumbling roads and bridges, schools and buildings within our own infrastructure.

Unfortunately, during the G.W. Bush administration, our leaders employed bad fiscal policies and showed great irresponsibility in the performance of their jobs. They were unproductive and their results are now leading our country into enormous debt and disorder.

For this malfeasance they should be jailed just as they would if they were running any big corporation.

Most of our representatives are only concerned with themselves. Of course, this is understandable, for it's a well-known fact that most thieves are self-centered and venal.

We've had our share of troubles: the ballot questions in the elections, and allowing the use of the Presidential Powers Act to make war with Iraq and Afghanistan in the Middle East. Those in power take advantage of that power.

And we have further fears: the loss of basic American freedoms and privacy caused by the G. W. Bush years and the creation of the Homeland Security, NSA, Patriot Act, Help America Vote Act, and the REAL ID Act.

As of this writing, this next Presidential election in 2020 will be extremely important to America. This time, those officials that we put in office can either further the freedoms we now enjoy, or they will continue down the path of a smaller, stronger and very secretive government, thereby creating more and more control over the people.

If "smaller and stronger" at the top happens, and our freedoms continue to be compromised, then the traditional checks and balances, the very protections provided by our Constitution and Bill of Rights may be lost forever.

A small group of government leaders will almost certainly cause greater losses of rights and liberties and could bring total oppression of the people eventually resulting in a dangerous totalitarian government.

Remember history. All tyrannical governments have been ruled by one leader, surrounded by a small group of loyal brigands who would unfailingly obey him.

Those people had no representatives, no voice and no Liberty. That's a dictatorship, my friends. Not freedom!

So what can we do? Well, first, we can let our governmental leaders know that we are watching them and we are not satisfied with their performance.

We must tell them what we need, and demand they take action to cure the many problems that exist.

Before the important mid-term elections, our incumbents and candidates must be aware of exactly what is necessary for them to if elected and to be firmly convinced that the American people want answers, not promises.

We must contact the political campaign leaders and let them know what the people want from their candidates.

These "campaign bosses" are the powerful chiefs who layout the campaign strategies and assist in designing the platforms of the parties. They have tremendous influence over the thinking of all local, state and national candidates.

If these campaign leaders hear what you have to say about the important major issues they could change the philosophy and direction of their candidates.

A bigger and more unified response from the people is necessary. To that end, I suggest that you go see them in person. And when you do, then telephone, write, email and fax your representatives with demands, and don't be meek!

Declare your position and stand-up and be heard.

Your voice must be listened to, loud and clear, so that the real issues are not again ignored.

Remember that *We, The People* are in charge of America.

The United States is still the greatest place on the face of the earth and our amazing country continues, flawed as it is, to expand and grow toward its goal of justice.

It is that quest and concept of excellence that historically has made us the envy of every nation in the world.

When the U.S.A. moves forward it sometimes slides back a little. But when those errors are corrected, we are often able to move even further ahead, and faster.

That's what we call American Progress, and we certainly don't want a few bad apples, our politicians, to spoil it.

Frederic Bastiat, a Frenchman once wrote:

> *When misguided public opinion honors what is despicable and despises what is honorable, punishes virtue and rewards vice, encourages what is harmful and discourages what is useful, applauds falsehood and smothers truth under indifference or insult, a nation turns its back on progress and can be restored only by the terrible lessons of catastrophe.*

Bastiat wrote that statement in 1850! It's a pretty good description of what is happening in America today.

The harm done by Bush and his gang of unmanageable and deceitful men, who started two wars and nearly brought down the economy of this country, will go down in history.

But those people are joined by Barak Obama's promises and his do-nothing administration that have given us all talk, and little action. Again, our country is in deep trouble.

Now we have Donald J. Trump as president. He is a con-man and fraudster who promises much, and delivers little.

Democrats or Republicans? Same pigs at the trough!

We must not forget that the cost of freedom is constant vigilance and total involvement in our government.

Don't be afraid to speak. Get motivated! Stop talking about your problems and fix them!

If the people speak-out and tell Them what We want, they must obey. We are in charge, not *Them*.

And, if they don't listen to us, they all should be fired and those who incumbent not elected again!

Idea: If any Representative fails to honestly speak for the people, he should be removed from office, and that if all in the Congress fail to represent the people, they ought to be removed from office, en masse, by force if necessary.

The following pages will give the mindset of our government, as well as, some of the Federal Bills they have sneaked by us, and made into law.

CHAPTER TWELVE

Law to Help the People

SINCE THE TERRIBLE DISASTER THAT occurred in New York City on September 11, 2001, Americans are frightened and have been told to be on constant "terrorism alert".

Few people realize that following that "9/11" tragedy our government, very conveniently, enacted some most insidious and oppressive laws in the history of our country.

In October of 2001, Congress unanimously passed *The Patriot Act.* This broadening of government surveillance powers was proposed to aid in the prevention of future foreign terrorist attacks.

In April of 2002 the *New Freedom Commission on Mental Heath* was established. This law will allow the government to test our children for mental stability and is intended to eventually be able to examine all U.S. citizens.

In December, of 2002 the *Help America Vote Act* was passed which allowed for Electronic Voting machines and Ballot Counting for all states.

In May of 2005, the *Real ID Act* was signed into law. This law allows our government to "number us" by issuing national identification cards for all citizens.

These new laws were, allegedly, intended to be helpful in providing benefits to American citizens. They are instead, by their nature, the obvious confirmation that a more powerful and authoritarian government has arrived.

Here are the summaries of these new Laws. I suggest that go to the internet and discover the further meanings.

THE PATRIOT ACT

The USA-Patriot Act is an acronym for "Uniting and Strengthening America" and "Providing Appropriate Tools Required to Intercept and Obstruct Terrorism."

That's a bullshit title, for a bullshit idea. Here is what all of that means to the citizens of the United States. After 9/11 Congress passed *The Patriot Act* to give new powers to the federal government in order to facilitate, investigate and arrest those they thought to be involved in terrorist activities.

The Patriot Act has been widely criticized for being too insidious and clandestine. It gives sweeping power to governmental agencies enabling them to monitor the personal habits of not only those identified as suspected terrorists, but anyone, including citizens, residing in the United States. It allows government agencies to spy, wiretap, open mail, and monitor email on all United States citizens residing abroad or in the United States who they believe might be, or could be, involved or affiliated with terrorism.

Airport Security machines. Drive-by Backscatter X-Raying. Cell phone surveillance. Internet surveillance... Our privacy is gone. Where will it end?

Freedom of speech began to erode with worries that the most innocuous of statements, particularly those made publicly, could lead to persecution and prosecution. We live in mortal fear of not being *Politically Correct*!

They can monitor the books you read, the places you go, the movies you see and draw their own conclusions.

These wide-sweeping powers allow the arrest of anyone, anytime and permit holding the arrested individuals indefinitely, without legal counsel.

Sound like the stories or movies we've seen about Nazi Germany? Well, now it's happening to us.

The president, George W. Bush, fanned the fires of fear in his November 6, 2001 speech by saying: "You're either with us or against us in the fight against terror." That comment was supposed to justify, and therefore make valid, the loss of most of our Constitutional rights.

The Patriot Act should be repealed! It may be too late. I don't know if whether can be stopped, but if the people speak out...

NEW FREEDOM COMMISSION
ON MENTAL HEALTH

When this Executive Order was first presented to the public in 2002, this plan for Better Mental Health seemed to be quite innocent in its design.

However, this national plan is based on a program created in 1995, called the Texas Medication Algorithm Project. Some critics contend that the drug industry influenced and backed the guidelines. Some consider that there is a "Political/Pharmaceutical" alliance afoot.

The potential "drugging of America" may be part of an insidious plan for controlling the people.

Here's a fact: The Big Pharma companies are the most profitable businesses in human history. Helping healthy people think they are sick is a huge business opportunity. Health experts might irresponsibly medicate children because they "seem to have mental problems." This could be compared to drug pushers getting kids hooked.

Here's how this could happen: A kid has a case of the terrible two's –they give him a pill. A fourteen-year-old son or daughter is acting irrational, like teenagers sometimes do–they give the kid a pill. An adolescent is depressed, thinks school sucks. Although it's just adolescence and peer pressure–the solution: a pill.

Imagine this scenario: At school, your kid is examined and declared emotionally troubled. The school authorities make recommendations. Prescriptions are ordered, and on the child's permanent record he or she is considered mentally unstable and must be medicated. By any standards, that becomes a career-limiting situation, but the kid is an ongoing customer for drugs!

Or, another scenario: You are watched at your job. If you stumble, or make a mistake, or talk back, you lose your job. Why? You are declared you emotionally erratic, mentally unstable. The diagnosis and the final report will be on your record for life. Not a pretty picture, is it?

It may be too late. I don' t know whether it can be stopped, but if the people speak out...

HELP AMERICA VOTE ACT

The HAVA bill, signed into law in 2002, calls for the use of electronic voting machines, in all states. These modern, stylish, yet fallible, machines have been used by many states. On the surface, they seem practical, a real help. But, there are certain problems with this technology that remain unsolved by our government.

Not all voting machines in use today have a paper trail. That's a paper receipt that could be used in the event of machine download failure or for a re-count of the votes. None of the manufacturers of these machines will allow any outsider to verify the accuracy of the software used in electronic voting. We are told that we must trust the accurateness of the manufacturer.

Since we all have heard that most computers can crash, programs can be clandestinely installed, and data can be hacked or manipulated, these machines are far from being trustworthy.

Yet we are told by our government not to worry.

It would seem to me that a logical request should be made to our government to thoroughly test the systems, before forcing us to use them. After all, our government requires test after test after test for their expensive weapons of war. Therefore, just as they test their war machines, the operating programs of these voting machines should be thoroughly examined in every way possible before they are foisted upon the American people.

The government should use outside contractors for testing and make public the results of each trial. Prove to us that these machines are, as they tell us, foolproof. Then, and only then, should Congress make a law for the mandatory use of this kind of equipment.

Rushing these Voting Machines untested and unverified into full operation has made the American people wonder if maybe *They* just might have an ulterior motive for *US*. Could our government intentionally want to manipulate our precious Vote in order to have further control over us?

Even considering the use of this faulty kind of technology one begins to understand that our Freedom and Liberty can easily be influenced and thereby lost forever.

The people must demand that our Representatives require all manufactures of this equipment to immediately and thoroughly test this electronic voting system and use the most stringent investigative procedures possible.

And by the way, as New York's Boss Tweed stated back in the 1870's, "As long as I count the votes, what are you going to do about it?" Guess that's the bottom line!

The window of opportunity to raise objections is quickly closing. But, maybe if the people speak out...

THE REAL ID ACT

There is a current government plan to issue new state drivers licenses to us, using mandatory Federal guidelines. This, of course, becomes a National ID card.

It seems that this new ID card will contain a tamper-proof micro chip with one or all of the following biometric security measures: Three photographs, including one that can only be seen under ultra-violet light, electronic DNA finger-prints, two retinal scans, full face imaging, possible DNA sampling and even more.

By swiping the metallic strip embedded in the card, a dossier and a list of recent activities, via purchases made by that individual, can easily be retrieved.

Requiring all citizens to be re-identified, and issuing a new high-tech permanent type ID card to each of us is surely coming in the very near future.

Will this new card stop the terrorists? Will the new card stop illegal immigration? Will it stop crime? I don't think so. Most criminals will quickly find a way to get a faked ID.

Why, then, does our government want to catalogue the good citizens of the United States along with criminals?

With all of the information on each of us stored in all of the computers, why would they want a new ID card?

The answer must be that they want to have a more uniform, up to date and easier access to information on us.

With the issues of immigration, the terrorist threat, etc. it is probably too late to stop the Real ID plan.

I don' t know if it can be stopped, but if the people speak out...

CHAPTER THIRTEEN

Declaring War

AND NOW, THE MOST IMPORTANT of all the issues:

Congress shall have the power to declare war.
ARTICLE 1, SECTION 8 OF THE US CONSTITUTION

Among the many circumventions and outright violations of our Constitution, war has been the most insidious.

The act of committing the United States military to direct war or the many interventions and police actions, hides the real reason for war: Profits!

Profits, not for the American people, but for the war profiteers, those that have existed since the founding of our country. They, and their cohorts in Congress, reap billions and billions of dollars if a war is declared or military actions are sanctioned by our government.

Throughout history, few politicians have ever fought in the wars they voted for, or created. They let the young die for a continuation of their power and profits, yet we elect these sadists and their like to office time and time again.

The United States has never been invaded in its history. The rest of U.S. warring has been contrived for dollars.

The early wars, including our so-called Revolutionary War, were merely wars to acquire land from Britain, Spain and France. They weren't about freedom, only conquest and profits for few, that were fought by the naïve military.

The wars thereafter were fought to keep and occupy other lands. Expelling those who challenged the U.S. power was considered patriotic.

Were they necessary? Worth dying for?

The Indians, the real owners of our land, watched as the white men killed each other in their wars of greed.

The Native American Indians believed the white man when he told them that he would co-exist with the Indians.

The white man lied and began in his uncontrollable avarice to want more and more of the Indian's land.

Then, during this out of control greediness, the white man committed overt genocide on the American Indians.

The near elimination of an entire race of people is an everlasting shame on America. It should never be forgotten.

Historically, our government has been ruthless.

Sometimes our military forces were loaned to help "other's causes" and sometimes they were used to reinforce our "political" and "commercial" interests.

The use of U.S. Military personnel for alleged, "just causes", "police actions" and "wars" since 1890 is amazing. As to whether these causes were "just", or even "necessary" is an ongoing subject for historians to debate.

The U.S. military, whether sanctioned by Congress, or not, has been quite busy exercising its mighty muscles during the last hundred years.

Our military has been actively protecting, attacking, intervening and occupying many countries for the good of our "national pride", as well as, the many American "corporate business interests" in those foreign countries.

Our politicians have employed the U.S. military as a kind of aggressive enforcer-type police department, and to paraphrase old Teddy Roosevelt, 'we do carry a big stick!'!

At home and abroad, the US military is to be feared!

In 1901 our government used the U.S. military to kill off a few dissident American Indians. In the 1920's they were used to beat-up American coal strikers and put down American rebellions. In 1932, between invasions and meddling, the Army stormed, killed and injured WWI vets in Washington, DC, who only wanted their War bonuses.

The big wars were fought for many of the same reasons as the little skirmishes. The U.S. needed to maintain their business and military power in various foreign lands. Believe it or not, it's been going on like that since the beginning of our country.

Is big business influencing the United States?

You see, GM, McDonalds, Coke, Ford, Apple, IBM and their like, couldn't set up shop in far-off countries if they didn't have the backing of the U.S. government and its military. With this backing their offers will not be refused.

Who would say no with the strength of the United States and its Military might looming over a deal.

By supporting these well-known corporations, the U. S. government acquired strong footholds in many countries.

And, it was all done under the auspice of "spreading freedom and democracy" to every country on the globe.

The former president of South Africa, Thabo Mbeki, stated the situation correctly:

You cannot export democracy. It has got to be homegrown, it has got to be indigenous. It is critically important that the people must have the space to determine their future. It does not matter how poor they are and how small they are. The idea that you have some super-powerful country which knows everything about everything is obviously wrong and obviously would never work.

But today the U.S. quest for power has gone too far. Now, more than ever, our corporations and politicians are using the United States military to take over countries,

They don't care what kind jeopardy they place on the rest of the world. Their actions are dangerous, ...and greedy.

Our government is completely out of control!

The United States seems to be on the path of aggressive world domination. Empire building?

So, what can we do help ourselves out of this mess?

Well here's an old idea. It's idealistic, and one that hasn't worked very well. But it has to be mentioned, so here goes.

First, we have to understand the problems facing us and then organize at a local level with family and friends. We need to stop talking and take action. Acta non verba.

We need to stop listening to the "Political Dogma" we are being fed and begin to research real facts about those people who want to be elected, or re-elected.

•Meet and talk with these candidates in person.
•Ask them questions.
•Put them on the spot.
•Make them prove that they are honest and trustworthy.
•Then call, write, mail, fax and email them.

Find out what these politicians will really do for the American People and make them commit to their promises. Give them pressure. Stay on their backs.

All elections are vitally important. Now is the time for you to come to the aid of your country.

Don't ever cast your valuable ballot for anyone you haven't researched. Find out if they are the best and why.

It's time to loudly give 'em hell and tell them what we want them to
do. They work for Us!

Be very sure If we don't, They will very soon be forcing Us to do
what They want, and that's a dictatorship.

And when it happens, you really won't like it.

CHAPTER FOURTEEN

A Message to the Politicians

YOU, OUR ELECTED LEADERS, MUST abide by the original conditions as set forth in the United States Constitution and the Bill of Rights. You have been elected to protect us. You must act as our representatives, not as our bosses.

When We The People speak to you, you must hear us and give us what we need for a better and safer life. You must be accountable. You must not lead us into jeopardy.

You work for us! You are the Servants of the American people. You are not our masters!

Clearly hear what the people want and then do the work we have elected you to do. Tend only to our business. There can be no "special interests" before us. We are number one.

Listen to what your constituents tell you, or we might recall you from your grand offices, possibly en masse, and by force if necessary. Revolution is in our DNA!

You must realize that 300 million of Us are quite able to rear-up, and that our criticism against an oppressive government is long overdue.

Presently, our government continues to gain power over We The People who for some reason remain Blithe, Blasé, and extremely Befuddled.

Wake up America!

However, the demand heaped upon us by our government grows stronger, and we grow weaker.

We must stop being frightened of our government.

By our numbers alone, They should respect and acknowledge our requests, ...or fear our reprisal!

Those representatives should think of their position in this way: If as a Congressman or Senator, I am not doing my job, I don't want American citizens pissed off at me!

No police force or standing army could save any of them from the 350+MILLION VERY ANGRY CITIZENS, who have banded together seeking to be heard.

They should be afraid. Very, very afraid!

In each election, the politicians asked to be hired, or re-hired. They will tell us anything to get elected.

Why would you hire anyone to work for you, if you knew nothing about him or her, except for what they have stated in their resume, or bragged about to you?

Before you committed to employing that person, you would do a background check, and if their record showed that they were not what they have represented themselves to be, you would not hire them.

This statement is just simple logic.

So, make a promise to yourself that you won't vote for anyone you haven't thoroughly researched. Find out who is asking for your vote and if they are worth considering.

Break the cycle of listening to what They say and doing what They tell you to do. We must think for ourselves.

Today, We, the People are again living in dangerous times. Some changes should immediately be made and until these things happen, there will be no fair elections, or good government for the American People.

Our Congress is still very selfish and ruthless.

Dwight D. Eisenhower, who had been the Supreme Allied Commander in WWII and directed the fight against fascism and national socialism, in his farewell address as President, Jan. 17, 1961 gently advised us:

In the councils of government, we must guard against the acquisition of unwarranted influence, whether sought or unsought, by the military-industrial complex. The potential for the disastrous rise of misplaced power exists, and will persist.

Now, whether you like his warning, or not, we have steadily become a fascist nation! Not by accident. By design.

The definition of fascism, according to most dictionaries:

A political ideology that seeks to combine radical and authoritarian nationalism with a corporatist economic system, which is usually considered to be on the far right of the traditional political spectrum.

One has only to look at the last administrations to learn that big corporations, have dramatically increased their wealth by using the wars, conflicts, actions, etc. and that our Congress has approved, and provided for them.

Corporate lobbying has influenced our representatives from their sworn duty to serve the American citizens by replacing honor and duty, with disgrace and treachery.

The window of opportunity to do something is closing faster that we know and what can we do to fix the many dangerous laws that are about to be introduced and soon inflicted on the citizens?

Five hundred and thirty five people in Congress control the standard of living and the destiny of over three hundred million people by using unbridled greed and power. Their authority over the people is inequitable and is not the intention of our founders. Nor, is it fair, just or honest.

Way back in 1949, George Orwell stated quite succinctly: Pretending that a true difference exists between the two major candidates is a charade of great proportion. Many who help to perpetuate this myth are frequently unaware of what they are doing and believe that significant differences actually do exist. Indeed, on small points there is the appearance of a difference. The real issues, however, are buried in a barrage of miscellaneous nonsense and endless pontifications by robotic pundits hired to perpetuate the myth of a campaign of substance. Influential forces, the media, the government, the privileged corporations and moneyed interests see to it that both party's candidates are acceptable, regardless of the outcome, since they will still be in charge. It's been that way for a long time.

Sadly, it is apparent that any effort in meeting, emailing, calling, demonstrating or even voting for an alleged "honest representative" is no longer possible. Maybe it never was.

Our representatives aren't listening, and they don't much care. Their honesty is in question. Most of what we are being told are lies. Consequently, they should all be fired!

Our government does not like it when we protest. We can do little to change the frightening circumstances we live in without committing to an organized uprising, and if our revolt is too intense and that definitely would be dangerous, for the government's response would be extremely violent.

Thomas Jefferson thought that a revolution against tyranny should made as often as was necessary.

Well, in 2009 a people's movement began. It was called The Tea Party, that, referring to the American colonists who dumped tea the harbor at Boston.

The Tea Party is a protest group that features as its core principal their Contract With [From] America. They are generally thought of as libertarians and conservatives and use the Gadsden (Don't Tread On Me) flag as their logo.

Most Tea Party members consider themselves to be the Republican Establishment.

Although they profess themselves as a 'grassroots' organization, many feel they are "astro-turfing". (pretending to be grassroots, but just being a part of a political party)

Not to be outdone, the Democrats and the Independents apparently did a little "astro-turfing", themselves.

In September of 2011 at New York City, protests against Wall Street caused similar protests to happen in major cities all across the country. They called it Occupy Wall Street.

Their statement was that the people were fed up with inequality and the rich controlling the country.

The people were speaking out again and this time they were doing something other than talking.

They made a general declaration entitled: A Public Statement from the New York City General Assembly Occupying Wall Street.

Have we forgotten what the relationship between our government and its people should be?

Remember: They, the government, are totally answerable to Us. Not we to them.

Dear Politicians:
We the People, are keeping an eye on YOU!

CHAPTER FIFTEEN

Summary

THE TEA PARTY AND OCCUPY WALL STREET. These two grass-roots movements are challenging the actions of our government and big business. A modern rebellion.

Whether either organization is successful or the movements of other future dissenting groups with their protests against the bankers, corporations and our government, only time will tell.

However, *We, The People,* must band together and rise up against tyranny. It will take all of us to make a difference.

President Trump has told us that he wants to "Make America Great Again." His idea is not to go forward, but to go back to a time of racial divide, misogyny and war.

Instead of bringing people together, he is dividing the nation by using his strange messages (the "tweets") and has trained his press representatives to lie and twist the facts.

As of this writing Donald J. Trump and his cronies are depriving the media, and the American people, of the truth.

An unfathomable man, Trump has made true weapons of confusion and misdirection. He's like no other president.

Trump could be compared to Mussolini and Hitler for his attempt to control the minds of the public. Of course, Il Duce and the Führer failed in their quest for power when the world nations united against them in World War II.

How are we to combat this rampant desire for sovereignty? Maybe, by using the old adage: Fight power with power.

*Impetus Improvisus ac violentus** might be the only idea remaining, however, we should try other means.

This is a recipe book. In it, you've gotten a potpourri of history for inspiration, a little dash of opinion and ideas, which if read, understood and used, could correct the ills that have befallen us.

The United States of America was founded by educated people who studied the successes and failures of many nations throughout history before they began their plan.

They had the good fortune to start a new nation conceived with justice and inalienable rights for all people.

The United States of America is the greatest example of liberty and freedom in all of history. We have had an opportunity like no other country before us.

I may have been cynical at times in this book for stating my personal opinion. Don't misunderstand me I love the U.S. of A and look forward to our country getting better.

In reality, America is a work in progress.

Unfortunately, and progressively, the intention to unravel the fabric that binds us is always a threat. We must not allow the citizens to become divided or we are doomed.

With the lying and false information given to us by our government leaders and the media, I certainly hope we don't become mindless and apathetic* and turn it all off.

If that happens we will, out of fear, or not caring, or not knowing, do what they tell us to do. We will be defeated.

Historically, humankind has not moved forward without taking action and fighting oppression.

Warning: If we do nothing this time we are most likely screwed. Sadly, even if we do something, it may be too late.

Given you a lot to think about and consider. Suggested much that you could and should do.

There you have it! I've done my duty, boys and girls.

So, goodbye now, ...and good luck to us all!

Definitions

Impetus Improvisus ac violentus

--LATIN: UNEXPECTED AND VIOLENT ACTION

Apathetic; Apathy

--DISPASSION, LETHARGY, INDIFFERENCE, LACK OF INTEREST, LACK OF ENTHUSIASM, LACK OF CONCERN

Acta Non Verba!

--LATIN: ACTIONS NOT WORDS

Epigrams

Rise like lions after slumber

in unvanquishable number.

Shake your chains to earth,

like dew which in sleep

had fallen on you.

Ye are many, they are few.

--PERCY BYSSHE SHELLEY

When Liberty is taken away by force,

it can be restored by force.

When it is relinquished voluntarily,

by default, it can never be recovered.

--DOROTHY THOMPSON

Imagine

BY JOHN LENNON

Imagine there's no Heaven

It's easy if you try

No hell below us

Above us only sky

Imagine all the people

Living for today

Imagine there's no countries

It isn't hard to do

Nothing to kill or die for

And no religion too

Imagine all the people

Living life in peace

You may say that I'm a dreamer

But I'm not the only one

I hope someday you'll join us

And the world will be as one

Imagine no possessions

I wonder if you can

No need for greed or hunger

A brotherhood of man

Imagine all the people

Sharing all the world

You may say that I'm a dreamer

But I'm not the only one

I hope someday you'll join us

And the world will live as one

ABOUT THE AUTHOR

STEVEN J. CONNERS was born in Dayton, Ohio. After nearly four decades in the entertainment industry, Conners "retired" to host a radio show, *The Voice of Reason*, in order to provide a platform for everyone's voice to be heard. His years of traveling the country and speaking with "the average person" inspired his recent fiction efforts, *The Madness of Power* series.

Conners worked in live theatre, creating, directing and producing numerous stage productions that traveled the United States, including *The Great Ghost Show* and *The Magic Land of Mother Goose*, before moving into the management and creation of event-style stunt promotions. In between tours and booking *Dilly the Dragon, The Six-Foot Chocolate Easter Bunny, The Magic Elf, Silkini's Frozen Alive* and *Silkini's Buried Alive*, Conners made a foray into designing and setting up several restaurants and even had a go at running a catering business (Shindigs Unlimited) and his own jazz club (Bozo's).

In addition to *The Madness of Power* series, Conners has written plays, children's books, a biography of showman Jack Baker, and a non-fiction book on the responsibilities of democratic liberty.

He continues to travel and maintains a home base in Reno, Nevada.

OTHER BOOKS BY STEVEN J. CONNERS:

THE MADNESS OF POWER Series

Book One: *No More Chances*
A story of Eco-Extremism

Book Two: *A-B-C*
Wars? Chaos? Overpopulation?
Why the answers are as easy as A-B-C.

Book Three: *Heaven on Earth* (Coming in 2018)
One Leader • One Government • One Language • One God
No Sickness or Death
Only Happiness and Eternal Life for Everyone

NON-FICTION

A Voice of Reason
A Handbook for Americans

Print and Kindle versions available at:

Amazon.com

Other ebook formats available at:

Smashwords.com

For author event information visit our website:

www.stevenjconners.com

www.ingramcontent.com/pod-product-compliance
Lightning Source LLC
Chambersburg PA
CBHW022111280326
41933CB00007B/344